PRAISE FOR
Saving the World Entire

"What wonder and wisdom is found here, what glorious and inspiring truth! These stories are the best of what has been taught for centuries of life's great truths."
—Neale Donald Walsch, author of *Conversations with God*

"The Talmud has withstood the test of time as one of the finest collections of parables ever assembled. *Saving the World Entire* will enrich the lives of all who read it."
—Jack Canfield, co-author of the *Chicken Soup for the Soul* series

"A readable and enjoyable book, culled from the charm and wisdom of the Talmud."
—Rabbi Norman Lamm, president, Yeshiva University

"These utterly beautiful parables from the Talmud are lessons for us all—Jews and Christians alike. They speak a prophetic truth drawn from divine inspiration. The wisdom of the Rabbis is a treasure for all people of faith."
—John Cardinal O'Conner, archbishop of New York

"A wonderful collection of parables and stories, each teaching unique values. Rabbi Bleefeld's comments both inform and elevate the reader. A window and gateway to the world of the Talmud. .   —Rabbi Sheldon Zimmerman,
president, Hebrew Union College

Rabbi Bradley Bleefeld holds one of the most prestigious positions in the American rabbinate as head of the Reform Congregation Keneseth Israel in Philadelphia, one of the nation's oldest and largest congregations. This is his first book. Rabbi Bleefeld lives in Philadelphia.

Robert Shook has collaborated
books. He lives in Columbus, O

SAVING THE WORLD ENTIRE

and 100 Other Beloved Parables from the *Talmud*

—◦◦◦—

Rabbi Bradley N. Bleefeld
and Robert L. Shook

Ⓟ

A PLUME BOOK

PLUME
Published by the Penguin Group
Penguin Putnam Inc., 375 Hudson Street,
New York, New York 10014, U.S.A.
Penguin Books Ltd, 27 Wrights Lane, London W8 5TZ, England
Penguin Books Australia Ltd, Ringwood, Victoria, Australia
Penguin Books Canada Ltd, 10 Alcorn Avenue, Toronto, Ontario, Canada M4V 3B2
Penguin Books (N.Z.) Ltd, 182–190 Wairau Road, Auckland 10, New Zealand

Penguin Books Ltd, Registered Offices: Harmondsworth, Middlesex, England

First published by Plume, an imprint of Dutton NAL,
a member of Penguin Putnam Inc.

First Printing, September, 1998
10   9   8   7   6   5   4   3   2   1

 REGISTERED TRADEMARK — MARCA REGISTRADA

LIBRARY OF CONGRESS CATALOGING-IN-PUBLICATION DATA:
Saving the world entire and 100 other beloved parables from the Talmud / [edited
    by] Bradley N. Bleefeld and Robert L. Shook.
        p.   cm.
    ISBN 0-452-27988-7
    1. Jewish parables.   2. Parables in rabbinical literature.   3. Talmud—
Parables—Translations into English.   I. Bleefeld, Bradley N.   II. Shook,
Robert L., 1938–   .   III. Talmud. English. Selections.
BM518.P3S28   1998
296.1'2760521—dc21   98-22127
                                                                 CIP

Printed in the United States of America
Set in Garamond

To my beloved wife, Merrie, who is beside me always,
and still listens to my stories.

—B.N.B.

In the memory of my dear friend, Jerome Schottenstein.

—R.L.S.

ACKNOWLEDGMENTS

This book was written as a labor of love, and while it took us nearly a year to complete, it took hundreds of years for others to compose. We are indebted to the sages and scholars of the Talmud, who over many centuries contributed to the text. It has been a humbling experience to write about the teachings of these extraordinary individuals.

Rabbi Bradley Bleefeld thanks his parents, Dorothy and Herman Bleefeld, who, as patient, devoted parents, rooted him in two worlds, the religious and the secular. He acknowledges his grandparents, Etta and Louis Bleefeld, and Celia and Harry Koenig, who introduced him to the pathways of the Talmud over four decades ago.

He also acknowledges his brother, Martin Bleefeld; Rabbi Jacob Alder, of the Young Israel of Kingsbridge in the Bronx; his mentor and friend, Rabbi David Goldstein; his friend, Rabbi Sam Joseph; teachers Rabbi Edward Goldman, Rabbi Richard Sarason, and Dr. Eugene Mihaly; his colleagues, rabbis David Stavsky, Alan Ciner, Areyah Kaltmann, Steven Engel, Stanley Davids, Mark Staitman, Stanley Miles, Eric Wisnia, Neal Borowitz, Henry Karp, and Gary Klein, for their wise advice and friendship; and dear friends Martha and David Rosner, Ron and Gail Kahn, and Joseph Zeigman.

Rabbi Bleefeld also expresses gratitude to his loving and caring machetunim, Dr. Gary and Nancy Schneider; his children, Rachel, Herschel, Marshall, and Amy for lovingly and patiently allowing and forgiving the consuming demands of his work.

Like the Talmud itself, this book was a collaboration, albeit on a minuscule scale, of many talented and devoted people. We thank our agent, Al Zuckerman of Writers House, who guided us to our publisher, Dutton Books. Al's inspiration and direction served us well from the beginning of this endeavor to its publication. Special thanks to Maggie Abel, Stormy Bailey, and Carla Keeton for their assistance in the transcribing, typing, and preparing of our manuscript. And another special thanks to Julia Serebrinsky, our editor, whose guidance and exceptional editing played a major role in the writing of this book.

CONTENTS

Introduction   1

SECTION I
A Path to Wisdom   5

Values   7
Insight   44
Fulfillment   57
Destiny   73

SECTION II
Living as a Community   81

Respect   83
Humility   107
Compassion   120
Harmony   142
Fairness   167

SECTION III

Our Covenant with God   187

Devotion   189
Faith   202

Conclusion   239

INTRODUCTION

Any introduction to the Talmud must start with a brief peek into history. When God gave Moses the Ten Commandments on Mount Sinai, Moses, in turn, passed them on to the Jewish people in the form of the Torah, the written law which became the first five books of the Old Testament. To explain the meaning of the written law, he also provided oral laws which too were passed on from generation to generation.

Talmud comes from the Hebrew word meaning "instruction." Over the centuries, however, the explanations became too numerous to commit them solely to memory, so it became necessary to preserve the oral law in writing. With the slaughtering of many scholars and rabbis during the reign of the Roman Empire, the need to preserve the law in writing became more urgent.

The sacred task of editing and arranging these laws in writing was undertaken by Rabbi Judah HaNasi, a Palestinian, who was known as Judah the Prince and lived around 200 C.E. With his colleagues, he compiled the work of many generations of rabbis who provided various explanations and legal interpretations. Judah HaNasi systematized the first layer of the text into six groups. They were called orders and pertained to the following subjects: (1) agriculture, (2) the Sabbath and festivals, (3) marriage, (4) civil and criminal law, (5) ritual sacrifices, and (6) cleanliness.

The orders are subdivided into 63 tractates, comprising 524 chapters, called the Mishnah, meaning the Second Law. Later, a series of commentaries and interpretations evolved around the text of the Mishnah; these comments and notes make up the second layer of the Talmud, called the Gemarah. Two versions of the Gemarah emerged: one was compiled in the fourth century by the scholars of Palestine, and another at the beginning of the fifth century by the scholars of Babylonia. These are respectively referred to as the Palestinian Talmud and the Babylonian Talmud.

Although it originated nearly 2,500 years ago, the Talmud is an encyclopedia of Jewish life that still encompasses every aspect of human experience. Its wide range of subjects covers everything from politics to poetry, folklore to civil law, marriage to math, history to science, and art to astronomy. The complete work touches all phases of secular and religious life.

Two kinds of literature appear in the Talmud: Halachah, which is the law, and Aggadah, which includes parables, stories, and sermons that illuminate the spirit of the law. The volumes of anecdotal material in the Aggadah contain rich layers of traditional Jewish values—lessons that are applicable to everyday contemporary life. While the Talmud is a considerable work, so much more than a collection of stories, the gems in *Saving the World Entire* were harvested from the Aggadah.

The wisdom of the Talmud is immense, and for centuries it has served as a primary source for rabbis and scholars, who devote a major portion of their daily lives to studying it. In Talmudic times, there were two great houses of learning. One was the school of Shamai, which urged a strict and unbending interpretation of the text. The other was the school of Hillel, and it was renowned for its more sympathetic take on the issues which the Talmud addresses. Consequently, when issues of scholarship and emotion arose, comparisons of the two schools' teachings often initiated impassioned debate.

Scholars have always said that one does not read the Talmud; instead, one becomes a student of it. The Talmud is an arduous document; its many lessons provide multifaceted explanations of the teachings. So, for this reason, it is referred to as an approach to reasoning.

With this in mind, *Saving the World Entire* will serve as a succinct introduction to the spiritual and intellectual foundation of the Talmud. We have selected a cross-section of parables on subjects ranging from the most serious matters to the most whimsical. Some parables are based on historical documents, while others are fables. We purposely picked a wide variety, because the sages of the Talmud often intermingled fact with fiction to illustrate their point. Above all else, these wise rabbis were wonderful storytellers prone to occasionally embellish their tales in order to teach the audience an important lesson. Often several lessons could be derived from the same story, and without a doubt every story could be interpreted in as many ways as these rabbis wished.

The writing of this book was a labor of love. We hope you will enjoy reading our favorite parables as much as we enjoyed researching and interpreting them.

SECTION I

—◦◦◦—

A Path to Wisdom

The Talmud emphasizes the interconnection between values, wisdom, and inner growth, and teaches lessons on how an individual can integrate them. The parables in this section are about the basic virtues and important insights a person should seek, and how this search can lead to a certain fulfillment and define destiny. Notice that the ancient sages were able to give extraordinary, timeless advice about how to perceive, interpret, and function in the world around us long before psychologists and authors of self-help books ever appeared. Their interpretations of the human condition are strikingly contemporary, and just as applicable today as they were centuries ago.

VALUES
1. Blind Man's Insight
2. The Fish and the Jewel
3. Alexander the Great Meets the Rabbis
4. The Sea Journey
5. Let the Lizard Beware
6. The Rabbi and the Throne

7. Taking a Backseat
8. The Poor, the Rich, and the Wicked
9. King Solomon's Doors
10. You Can't Eat Gold
11. In Search of Oil
12. The Ugly Bride
13. The Rope
14. The Value of Friendship
15. A Place Called Honesty
16. A Test of Strength
17. Saving the World Entire

INSIGHT
18. The "Dead" Lizard at the Banquet
19. The Old Man and the Fig Tree
20. Word Games
21. The Doubting Fisherman
22. Real Jewels
23. The Emperor's Daughter and the Ugly Scholar

FULFILLMENT
24. In Pursuit of Scholarship and Riches
25. It's Always Something
26. The King and Eye
27. The Inner Voice
28. The Rabbi and the Harlot
29. Steel on Steel
30. The Joy of Sabbath

DESTINY
31. The Rains Came
32. The Death of the Great Sages
33. A Fish Out of Water

VALUES

———— ❦ ————

1. Blind Man's Insight

On a certain day, the king of Israel was expected to travel through the village, and all the villagers gathered to see him go by. Although blind, Rabbi Sheshet joined the others as they waited patiently for the king's arrival.

Knowing that the great rabbi was blind, a cynic said, "People take whole pitchers to the river to fetch water, but of what use is it to take a broken pitcher to the river?" The blind rabbi understood what the man's negative remark really meant: what's the point of a blind person waiting to see the king?

Rabbi Sheshet answered, "Foolish man! I will demonstrate to you that not only will I know when the king arrives, but I am capable of understanding what is happening better than you who have vision."

When a legion of soldiers appeared, the cynic joined the crowd in shouting, "The king is coming!"

"No, he isn't," the blind rabbi said. And, as predicted, the legion passed by without the king.

A second legion marched down the road toward the center

of the village, and again the cynic and the crowd shouted, "The king is coming!"

Again, the rabbi said the king was not coming, and once more that turned out to be true.

A third legion marched by, and this time the crowd fell silent. But Rabbi Sheshet exclaimed, "Now the king is coming!"

When he saw the king, the puzzled cynic asked, "How were you able to tell?"

The rabbi answered, "We learn from scripture that once, long ago, Israel waited for God to pass by. When a powerful wind blew through the mountains, even giant rocks were shattered to small stones, but the Lord was still not in the wind.

"Then after the wind, an earthquake came. But God was not in the earthquake. Then there came a fire, but the heavenly Sovereign was not in the fire.

"After the fire," the rabbi continued, "a still, small voice was heard, and God was found in that hush. It was the hush of today's crowd that informed me that the king was coming."

As the procession passed by, Rabbi Sheshet offered an appropriate blessing for the king he could not see, but the cynic understood that the blind rabbi was indeed also blessed.

[TALMUDIC SOURCE: *Berachot 58*]

Rabbi's Comment:

This parable teaches that all human beings have value which can either be conspicuous or hidden. Those who struggle with physical and psychological challenges are often blessed with heightened powers of understanding and sensitivity. These special individuals often manifest a greater appreciation for the world and its beauty and order because of the exceptional effort they must exert to discern the environment around them.

Though he was blind, Rabbi Sheshet's intellect and keen powers of discernment enabled him to have more insight than others whose senses were intact. The second lesson here is that we should never take the blessings such as sight, hearing, and health for granted.

2. The Fish and the Jewel

A gypsy fortune-teller once told a man of meager means: "Be careful! A very rich man named Joseph, who always honors the Sabbath day, will someday own all of your possessions."

To prevent the fortune-teller's prediction, the man devised a plan. He sold everything he owned, and with the money, he bought a precious gem. To keep his valuable new possession in safety, he hid it in the turban that he never took off his head.

One day while the man was crossing a bridge, a strong wind blew off his turban, and it fell into the stream below. Just then a fish swam by and swallowed the hidden jewel. The same fish was caught and sold on the market as the freshest and best catch of the day. "Who will buy this fine fish?" the villagers cried.

"Go to Joseph," someone suggested. "Certainly he will purchase this beautiful, fresh fish for the Sabbath."

Joseph was delighted to buy the fish because he always wanted the best and freshest fish for the Sabbath. When he cut the fish open, to his great surprise, he found the precious gem inside and later sold it for a large sum of money.

The story about Joseph and the fish spread from village to village. In response, a wise old sage said, "Whosoever spends for the Sabbath, the Sabbath has a way to pay him back."

{TALMUDIC SOURCE: *Shabbat 119a*}

Rabbi's Comment:

This parable teaches that while limited resources may make it necessary to scrimp and save all week to allow for a more extravagant celebration of the Sabbath, those who observe it appropriately will find a reward. Though this reward may not be in the physical form of a gem, its value will be derived from the new energy which the observance of Sabbath will bring.

3. Alexander the Great Meets the Rabbis

It has been written that Alexander the Great enjoyed challenging the rabbis in debate and discussion. On one occasion, he interrogated a group of rabbis with a series of thought-provoking questions.

"Who is wise?" he challenged.

The rabbis huddled together, and after a moment their leader replied, "One who can anticipate the future."

"Who is strong?" Alexander inquired.

"The person who can control his temper," one of the rabbis quickly answered.

"Well," said the powerful conqueror, "tell me then who is rich."

"The rich person is the one who is satisfied with his portion," one of the rabbis said.

"And what should a person do to live a full life?"

Again the rabbis gathered in a small circle, and following a short debate, a spokesperson told the emperor, "A person should kill himself with study and hard work."

Confused by the unusual answer, Alexander said, "So what then should a person do to die?" he asked.

"Rather let him keep himself alive with the ways and means to ease his life," he was told.

"And how should a ruler become popular?" he asked.

"The people have a disdain for control, so a ruler should respect each individual's love for freedom," the rabbis answered.

"Ha!" Alexander exclaimed. "I have a better answer." In a deep, authoritative voice, he bellowed, "Let a ruler love power and control, and at the same time, bestow goodness on the people."

"I have one more question to ask," the mighty ruler declared. "Is it better to live on the water, or to live on dry land?"

"Dry land," the rabbis all agreed.

One rabbi explained, "Because those who journey by sea are never fully calm until they reach dry land, their destination."

[TALMUDIC SOURCE: *Tamid 32a*]

———❧———

Rabbi's Comment:

Although we can only speculate about whether this dialogue actually took place, some parables in the Talmud teach lessons by using the most powerful individuals of their time as examples.

In this parable, the Talmud reminds us that wisdom, contentment, and personal freedom were just as much at the forefront of our concerns in the past as they are today. This parable is also a reminder that in order to feel secure, we must build our lives on a solid foundation. From the rabbis' point of view, this foundation is the solid strength of Torah and the values it teaches. The interpretations of these precepts by Talmudic scholars guides us in applying God's laws and commandments to everyday life. Living each day according to the laws of the Torah builds a life of substance and value. Only the realization of this goal insures lasting contentment.

———❧———

4. The Sea Journey

Rav Judah enjoyed telling his students about the sea journey from India, his homeland, to Israel.

"After several days at sea," Rav said, "I saw a large shining object on the ocean floor. Immediately, the crew and I declared it to be a precious gem. Although a sea serpent lurked nearby, a diver attempted to retrieve the jewel.

"Suddenly, the monster charged the ship. Its mouth gaped wide, and without a doubt, the monster was about to swallow the ship. However, thanks to our good fortune, a huge black condor swooped down from the sky and bit off the sea serpent's head. The water around us turned red with blood.

"Out of nowhere, another sea serpent appeared. It carried the severed head to its mate and reattached it, restoring the monster's life and its fury. Now it was even more intent on devouring the ship. Again, our lives were gravely endangered.

"But then the condor flew down and bit off the monster's head. By this time, the diver had thrown the jewel onto the ship's deck.

"It just so happened the ship contained a large store of salted birds. Incredibly, as the jewel rolled near, each bird came to life. Finally, all of the salted birds flew away, taking the jewel with them.

"It was a miracle that we all survived."

[TALMUDIC SOURCE: *Baba Batra 74b*]

—◦⦙◦—

Rabbi's Comment:

The rabbis were superb storytellers, and they often entertained their students with tall tales. On many occasions, they were given to exaggeration and took great license in making a point—as indicated in Rav Judah's story. Here a sea serpent symbolizes the evil forces of the netherworld bent on our destruction. The black condor and birds represent the salvation of Heaven.

The jewel stands for the secrets of life eternal. Each individual journeys through life seeking truth. Often, the truth seems like it's within our grasp, only to become elusive and unavailable as we approach it. Rav Judah used this story to encourage his students to continue searching for the truth, reminding them not to be deterred by difficulties they will encounter along the way.

—◦⦙◦—

5. Let the Lizard Beware

An oversized, ornery lizard dwelled in the crevasses of a dilapidated wall in the outskirts of the village. The lizard loved jumping out at passers-by and took immense pleasure in frightening people. On occasion, it would even bite small children.

Eager to put an end to this terror, a group of villagers went to Rabbi Hanina Ben Dosa, whose wisdom was widely acknowledged, hoping that he would have a solution.

When the rabbi heard of the mischievous lizard's actions, he demanded, "Take me to this vile, despicable creature, and I will put an end to his meanness."

The villagers led him to the wall. There Rabbi Hanina spotted a hole through which the lizard's dark eyes glared. As the rabbi tried to put his heel over the hole, the lizard jumped out and bit his foot. The lizard then rolled over and died.

Rabbi Hanina picked up the dead carcass by the tail and flung it over his shoulder. When he arrived at his house of study, he summoned his students and announced, "Look here, my boys! It is not the lizard that kills, but rather sin that kills."

For years thereafter, the villagers would say, "Woe is the person who is unfortunate enough to meet up with a mean-spirited lizard. But woe is to the lizard who is unfortunate enough to meet up with Rabbi Hanina Ben Dosa!"

[TALMUDIC SOURCE: *Berachot 33a*]

Rabbi's Comment:

In this parable, the lizard represents the sins of conscience: meanness, arrogance, and disregard for the well-being of others. Rabbi Hanina is the hero who triumphs over evil, and in doing so, he teaches a meaningful lesson to his disciples. When a good person faces adversity and prevails, it serves as a reminder to others that goodness can triumph over evil in their lives too. Though not always the case, goodness must be viewed as stronger than evil so that a flicker of hope can always remain.

6. The Rabbi and the Throne

When Rabbi Judah was asked to appoint a judge and teacher for the village of Simonia, he picked the learned Rabbi Levi Bar Sissi for the job.

The townspeople were so excited about the impending arrival of their new rabbi and scholar that they constructed a platform on which he could sit in a special, elevated chair and they could gather around him in reverence.

After the city extended its grand welcome, Rabbi Levi Bar Sissi was ushered onto the platform where he was to hold court. Once he was seated, the villagers began to ask him questions. Unfortunately, after hearing the first three questions, he had no answers to give. It was an embarrassing moment for him. Although normally he would have responded to each question with considerable ease, on this day his mind was a complete blank. He could only say, "I'm sorry, but I can't answer your three questions. Does someone else have another question to ask?" Alas, the disappointed crowd dispersed. The poor rabbi slumped in despair.

The following morning, he went to visit his mentor. After one look at him, Rabbi Judah knew that Rabbi Levi Bar Sissi was deeply troubled. "What have the good people of Simonia done to cause you such distress?" he asked.

"My dear teacher, Rabbi Judah," he bemoaned, "the people of Simonia asked me three questions, but the answers escaped my mind. I can't believe it. Although I knew each of the answers before I arrived in town, once there, I was unable to think of a single answer."

"What were the questions?" Rabbi Judah inquired.

Without hesitation, Rabbi Levi Bar Sissi quickly rattled off each question, following each one with a brilliant answer.

"You know the answers very well," Rabbi Judah said. "So why didn't you state them yesterday in Simonia?"

"My teacher, when I was lifted to the platform by the good people of Simonia and I sat upon the tall chair, it was as if I were on a throne. I was so overwhelmed by the people's reverence, the answers escaped my mind."

In his wisdom, Rabbi Judah asserted, "Let this serve as an example to you, and to all who aspire to rabbinic leadership in their communities. If you are consumed with pride and have lost humility, your knowledge will abandon you."

[TALMUDIC SOURCE: *Bereshit Rabbah 81*]

━━◦◦◦━━

Rabbi's Comment:

When others revere us, we must not, in turn, idolize ourselves. Truly great people are not influenced by the adulation of others. Instead, they remain humble and aware that they possess frailties and blemishes unseen by their admirers. They maintain proper perspective by not allowing pride to distract them from their real work. Those who lose their humility also lose the very foundation upon which others pay tribute to them.

━━◦◦◦━━

7. Taking a Backseat

At a gathering where the community of villagers congregated, the rabbis had taken seats together in the front row.

Arriving a few minutes late, Rabbi Nahman Ben Isaac took a seat in the rear of the hall.

One of his colleagues spotted him there and called out, "Rabbi Nahman! Come up closer to the front and take a more prominent seat with us. A man of your learning should not have to sit in the back row."

"Thank you for the invitation," Rabbi Nahman answered. "While it would be an honor to sit with you, I am content where I am. After all, have we not been taught, 'It is not the place that gives honor to the person, but the person who gives honor to the place.' "

Having said that, Rabbi Nahman sat down, and all who were present were reminded that humility was his claim to greatness.

[TALMUDIC SOURCE: *Ta'anit 7a*]

Rabbi's Comment:

A person of true merit doesn't need to occupy a special place of honor; it is his presence that enhances the place. Rabbi Nahman also reminds us that a person with sufficient self-esteem does not always have to be in the limelight, but feels at ease even when he "takes a backseat" to others.

8. The Poor, the Rich, and the Wicked

On the day of reckoning, everyone must account before the heavenly court. It matters little what position a person attains in life; whether the person is rich, poor, or wicked, the question is always the same: "Why didn't you spend time in study, striving always to seek knowledge?"

It is common for a poor person to answer, "I did not study because I was so poor that I had to spend my time doing whatever work I could find in order to sustain my family and myself."

The court would then reply, "Nobody was any poorer than Hillel. And Hillel, the elder, would sometimes work all day for a tarpick. He was known to give half of his meager wages to the guard at the house of learning to assure his admittance. He kept the remaining half to support his family.

"On one occasion when Hillel had been unable to find work for some time, the guard refused to allow him to enter the study house without paying. This prompted Hillel to climb onto the roof, where he sat by the skylight to hear the wisdom of God being spoken by the two great masters, Shemayah and Avtalyon.

"According to legend, it was a cold winter Sabbath evening, and before long, Hillel was covered with three feet of snow. Upon discovering him the following morning, Shemayah and Avtalyon retrieved Hillel's frozen body and brought him inside. There they gave him a hot bath, bundling him in warm blankets near the fireplace.

"'Avtalyon, my brother,' Shemayah said, 'this man deserves our highest admiration because he possesses an insatiable desire to learn. He is so deserving that even the Sabbath ought to be transgressed on his behalf.'"

Similar to the poor man, a rich man commonly defends his

lack of study by saying, "Because I was so rich, I had to occupy myself with the protection of all my possessions."

The court would say to such a person: "Certainly you were not as rich as Rabbi Eliezer, the son of Harsom, who was left an inheritance of a thousand villages. He also was left an equal amount of ships at sea. His servants managed his business affairs while he went from village to village each day so he could study all the laws of the Torah. He carried a sack of flour on his back to make his meals when he was away from home.

"In one city, he was not recognized, and his own servants forced him to perform public labor. Rabbi Eliezer pleaded for his release so that he could be free to study the law and continue his education.

" 'No! By the name of our master, Rabbi Eliezer Ben Harsom, we will not let you go,' they told him.

"Only after he was able to convince them of his identity was he released. For the rest of his life, Rabbi Eliezer continued his study of the Torah."

And when the wicked man is asked why he did not find time to study, he says it was because he was preoccupied with his own beauty and passion.

To the wicked, the heavenly court would answer, "In all the world, surely no one was more beautiful than Joseph. Yet when Potiphar's wife tried to seduce him, Joseph did not give in to the temptation, because it would distract him from his study of the Torah. And oh, how she tried to sway him. She repeatedly told him how much she desired him. She wore revealing clothes, offered him one thousand silver coins, and finally threatened to put him in prison, where he must perform hard labor and endure severe torture. Still, he refused to succumb to her passion. Joseph never allowed Potiphar's wife, or anyone else who was attracted to him for his physical beauty, to interfere with his desire for study and intellectual growth. He refused to compromise his respect for the Torah."

These examples of Hillel, Rabbi Eliezer, and Joseph remind us that there is no excuse for any of us to neglect our commitment to study and to gain knowledge.

[TALMUDIC SOURCE: *Yoma 35b*]

———※———

Rabbi's Comment:

The rabbis loved to teach, and one of their favorite ways to do so was by comparison. Here, they compare the answers of three different individuals who respond to the metaphorical question of why they didn't take time to study, when, in fact, they did have many opportunities.

As these three examples show, the quest for material sustenance, the possession of enormous wealth, or the desire for passion should never consume so much of our time that we are unable to develop our minds and continually grow.

———※———

9. King Solomon's Doors

God gave the honor of building the first Temple in Jerusalem to King Solomon, the third king of Israel and son of the Great King David. His wisdom for architecture was legendary; his insight into design beyond compare. But in the land of Israel, building materials were very limited. King Solomon wished to embellish the great structure with precious metals and exotic accessories, so he sent a man named Nicanor to Alexandria in Egypt to secure two bronze doors for the Temple.

Nicanor boarded a ship with these doors and sailed homeward. During his journey, a thunderous storm imperiled the ship. Fearing for their lives, and hoping to calm the waters, the sailors threw one of the doors into the sea. The storm, however, continued, and the sea boiled over across the ship's deck. Again the crew hoped to appease the storm by throwing the matching door overboard. At this point Nicanor protested, wrestling the door away from the crew.

"Throw me in with it," he yelled.

Without hesitation, they obliged him.

Suddenly, the storm abated. Nicanor and the door floated nearby and were hauled aboard by the sailors. Nicanor, thinking that his mission had failed and feeling miserable, watched as they neared the port of Acco with only a single door. But as the ship docked, an incredible thing happened. The other door bobbed up beside the ship amid raging waters. According to legend, a sea monster spit the door onto dry land.

The resurrection of the door prompted Solomon to reconsider the Temple he was building in Jerusalem. He observed that all its beams were made of cedar wood, and all its walls were of cypress. Furthermore, the gates of the sanctuary were all made of gold, with the exception of the doors of Nicanor.

Yet these doors, although made of bronze, glowed miraculously as if they too were made of pure gold.

[TALMUDIC SOURCE: *Yoma 38a*]

Rabbi's Comment:

The rabbis liked legendary stories with exaggerated
details that spiced up their lessons. Many contained
creatures and monsters that could cause or obliterate a
storm, turn day into night, and so on. Here, Nicanor's
special doors were designated to stand in a distinct place
in Solomon's Temple because they inspired miracles.

10. You Can't Eat Gold

During the siege of Jerusalem, the rabbis asked the Biryoni, a band of zealous defenders, to make peace with the Romans. But the Biryoni refused, vowing to resist their conquerors.

"You will not succeed," the rabbis warned, "and we are doomed."

Consequently, believing a famine would garner public support, the Biryoni torched the city's grain silos.

Martha, daughter of Behthius, was one of Jerusalem's richest women. She told her servant, "Go buy some fine flour." The servant could find only coarse white flour, so he returned without the fine flour.

"Then get some coarse white flour," she ordered.

But the course white flour was gone by then, and only the dark flour was available. When the servant returned to his mistress empty-handed, Martha sent him back for dark flour; this time only barley flour was left. When Martha sent him to buy barley flour, he found it all gone.

Martha had already removed her shoes for the day, but she said, "I will go myself and see what I can buy." But as she searched, she became weak and feverish and realized she was dying.

Martha managed to get home, where she gathered up all her gold and silver and threw it onto the street. "What good are these things to me?" she cried.

Thus, the prophecy of Ezekiel was fulfilled, "They shall cast out their silver possessions into the streets," for without food, the most precious possessions are worthless.

[TALMUDIC SOURCE: *Gittin 56a*]

Rabbi's Comment:

The ongoing Jewish rebellion against the Romans provides the historical context for this lesson. The siege and subsequent famine highlight the disparity between material possessions and the need for life's real essentials. When life and health are threatened, ownership of material objects becomes meaningless. Even in the best of times, gold and silver simply enhance well-being; they cannot sustain it. Pursuit of wealth alone cannot bring true happiness.

This does not suggest it is sinful to enjoy little luxuries if one has the means to obtain them. Dedication to their pursuit, however, is frivolous and foolish. One must realize that life can be full without material luxury as long as one has the luxury of good health and happiness. Martha's sad fate reminds us to carefully consider what we truly value.

11. In Search of Oil

It was a sad day in Ladakiya when the town had exhausted its oil supply. Quickly, the townspeople appointed a buyer to tour the nearby villages in search of this precious commodity. He was given a purse large enough to buy oil for the entire community.

The buyer's first stop was Jerusalem, where he encountered disappointment. In the holy city, every dealer gave the same reply: "We don't have enough oil to spare some for Ladakiya. See if Tyre can supply your oil."

At Tyre, he heard the same story. "We barely have enough oil for our own needs. We suggest you travel to Gush Halav."

The buyer was given a ray of hope in Gush Halav when a stranger advised him: "Only one man can sell you such a large quantity. You'll find him working in the fields." The buyer was directed to the fields, where he found a man covered with sweat and dirt, digging around his olive trees.

The buyer was aghast. Surely, he thought, this cannot be the supplier I was urged to see. This grimy, dirty man is obviously a common laborer.

The buyer greeted the worker cautiously. "I have been sent to buy oil for my entire village," he told the man. "Is it possible you have such a large supply to sell me?"

"Please let me finish my work," the laborer replied. "Then we will talk."

The buyer watched the sky grow dark while the digging was completed. At last, the laborer gathered his tools and nodded to his visitor.

"Come with me," he said. "At my house we will discuss what I can do for you."

As the buyer followed, the man cleared the path before

them. This is a waste of time, the Ladakiyan thought to himself. But what else can I do? I suppose I must go with him.

As the men approached the house, a servant rushed out with a hot bowl of water. The servant kneeled before the host and washed his hands and feet. Another servant came forward with a golden bowl of oil, into which he dipped his master's hands and feet to soothe them.

Then the buyer was invited to sit down and dine. After the meal, he was asked how much oil was needed.

"That seems inadequate for an entire town," the host commented.

"Actually, we could use more," his guest replied, "but I can only pay for the amount I have requested."

"Do not worry," said his host. "We will take as much as you need. I will accompany you to Ladakiya. After delivering the oil, the town can pay me the balance."

When the two men left Gush Halav, it has been said that there was not a single horse, mule, camel, or donkey that remained idle in all of Israel. All were hired to transport this generous cargo.

The anxious townspeople of Ladakiya swarmed forward to greet the two as they reached the city gates. They thanked and praised the stranger for supplying them with the desperately needed oil. After receiving his payment, the man departed.

The Talmud repeats the moral of this parable as it appears in Proverbs: There are those who appear to be wealthy, but have nothing; and there are those who appear to be poor, but have great wealth.

[TALMUDIC SOURCE: *Menachot 85b*]

Rabbi's Comment:

Here the rabbis wish to teach the elementary lesson that things are not always as they seem. The laborer in the field hardly appears to be a wealthy man; later, however, the evidence of his wealth is revealed. In fact, his enormous reserve of oil implies that he has enormous wealth. Sometimes the truth about a person lies beneath the surface, and a little digging might reveal that truth.

12. The Ugly Bride

A marriage arrangement was made on behalf of a man and a woman who were to meet for the first time on their wedding day. Unfortunately, when the big day finally came, the man took a look at his bride-to-be and declared her so ugly that he refused to marry her.

It was an embarrassing moment. The poor bride was humiliated, and both families were upset, but no one knew what should be done. The groom realized he must do something. After some deliberation, he announced what he thought was a reasonable solution.

"I will not marry you," he said to her in front of everyone, "until you prove to me that you have at least one fine quality." A gleam of hope appeared in the bride's eyes, and she nodded through her tears.

Since Rabbi Ishmael, one of the greatest judges of that time, attended the wedding, the groom decided to seek his counsel and to abide by his decision, whatever it might be.

The rabbi agreed to the arrangement and began to question the man.

"Tell me, is your bride's head beautiful?" Rabbi Ishmael asked.

"No. In fact, it is as round as a watermelon," the man answered.

"Well, is her hair beautiful?"

"Not at all. It is like rough unwoven flax."

"Well, perhaps her eyes are pretty," the rabbi said.

"Absolutely not! They are cloudy and bleary."

"Could it be that she has a nice nose?" the rabbi questioned.

"No." The man sighed. "Her nose is crooked and misshapen."

"What about her lips?"

"Swollen."

"And her neck?"

"Hunched."

"Her stomach?"

"It protrudes."

"Perhaps she has attractive feet?" the rabbi suggested.

"They are as wide as the feet of a duck," the man replied, shaking his head.

As a last resort, Rabbi Ishmael asked, "What about her name? Is her name also defective?"

Someone in the back called out, "Her name means repulsive!"

"Enough!" Rabbi Ishmael said. "In my estimation she is a fitting bride for you, and the ceremony should begin at once."

"B-b-but how can that be?" the man stammered.

"Because her name is an honest reflection of her physical characteristics," Rabbi Ishmael replied. "Surely, she could have changed her name. She did not, however, which indicates she is a woman with integrity and fine character. She will make a fitting partner in this marriage."

"You are right, Rabbi, and I am indebted to you for your insight!" the groom exclaimed. "I wish to marry her immediately!"

The couple was married and lived happily ever after.

[Talmudic source: *Nedarin 66b*]

Rabbi's Comment:

The rabbis always taught not to judge people by their outer appearance, but rather to appreciate their inner worth. Rabbi Ishmael knew that beauty was only skin deep, and in this particular case, the bride's truly important qualities lay beneath the surface.

The Talmud teaches that one should not be deceived by appearances, but instead should explore the potential treasure that lies within each person.

In a marriage, honesty and integrity rather than pleasing facial features are the true building blocks of a long, rich relationship. Living a life of respect and patience toward yourself and your mate helps to assure a fulfilling partnership.

13. The Rope

When Rabbi Huna was a young man, his good friend, Rav, noticed him wearing a rope around his waist.

"What a strange sight you are," Rav said, "with that rope."

"I had no money to buy wine so I could make a blessing on the Sabbath," Huna replied. "Therefore, I pawned my decorative belt, and now I must wear this rope."

"Well, my friend," Rav said, "may the day come when Heaven will bless you with such riches that you will be smothered in silk."

Years passed, and Huna acquired considerable fortune. On the wedding day of his son, Rabbah, Huna became drowsy shortly after the ceremony. He curled up on a couch to take a nap.

Now Huna was a slight man, so when Rabbah's bride and sisters came to change from their wedding finery, they did not see Huna. They removed their silk garments and threw them on top of the sleeping man, and shortly, Huna was indeed covered with silk. Upon awakening to find himself smothered in silk, he realized that his colleague's prophetic words had come true.

When Huna related this story to Rav, his old friend laughed with delight.

"So," Rav replied, "why did you not also bless me with the same good fortune? For I, too, would have been pleased to be smothered in silk!"

[TALMUDIC SOURCE: *Megillah 27b*]

Rabbi's Comment:

This parable teaches us not to rely on material possessions for a sense of well-being, or to dismiss or rebuke a person for his situation in life. Fortunes change, and riches wax and wane as we make our way through life's passages. And when we have endured a tough financial predicament, there is no reason to feel disgrace. Note, too, a true friend will always offer prayers for our prosperity and well-being.

14. The Value of Friendship

"My dear friend, Rabbi Joshua, I haven't seen you for more than thirty days. What shall I say to you?"

"You should say a blessing," the rabbi answered.

"But which blessing would be appropriate?"

"The most apropos would be, 'Blessed is the One who has kept us alive, sustained us, and brought us to this occasion.' "

"That is a fine blessing," the man replied. "But what if a year had elapsed since I had seen you? Then what should I have said?"

"In such a situation, say, 'Blessed is the One who revives the dead.' "

"Revives the dead?" the man questioned. "How could that be? The dead are generally not forgotten until after a year."

"That is indeed true," the rabbi said. "But if you haven't seen or heard from a friend for more than a year, you might as well count him as one who has died."

[TALMUDIC SOURCE: *Berachot 58*]

Rabbi's Comment:

This parable reminds us not to take our friends for granted. There is a tendency to become so involved in our daily lives that we lose sight of the true bonds we have with others. As Rabbi Joshua teaches, we should not allow a lapse of time to stop us from thinking about the well-being of our dear ones.

By offering a prayer, we express our joy at seeing a

friend following a period of separation. Although time has passed, we express gratitude for both our friend's well-being and for the relationship that has remained intact.

15. A Place Called Honesty

Rabbah, the great teacher, said, "Once I believed there was not a person in the world who was completely truthful. But that was before I heard the story of Reb Tabut, a man so honest that if he could obtain all the riches in the world by telling a lie, he would refuse.

"Reb Tabut once came to a village called Kushta, which means 'honesty.' Kushta received its name because the people who lived there never told a lie; in addition, no one there ever died before his or her time.

"Reb Tabut fell in love with a woman who had two sons. He married the woman and for years enjoyed a happy life with her. One day, while his wife was bathing, a neighbor knocked on the door and asked to see her. To her husband, it was a matter of etiquette and modesty when he answered, 'She is not here right now.'

"As a result of this falsehood," Rabbah continued, "he was punished by the death of his wife's two sons. When the townspeople heard what happened, they accused him of bringing death to their doorsteps. As punishment, he was ordered to leave their village and was forbidden to return."

[TALMUDIC SOURCE: *Sanhedrin 97a*]

Rabbi's Comment:

We can never be certain about the repercussions of the lies we tell. We are often unaware that our remarks have significant impact on others and that people can act on what they may believe is the truth. In this parable, what appeared to be an innocent fabrication resulted in tragic consequences. Hence, the Talmud teaches us to be mindful of the truth, because no matter how trivial we think our lies may be, they can significantly change the lives of others.

16. A Test of Strength

"There are ten strong elements in the world," Rabbi Judah lectured his students, "and each is capable of being stronger than another. Still, the mightiest strength of all is the ability to perform a good deed."

"Teacher," one student said, "this sounds perplexing. How can a good deed be the strongest element in the universe?"

"I will explain," Rabbi Judah told them. "A rock is hard, but isn't it true that an iron blade can cut it in two? And although iron is hard, the heat from a flame softens it. Likewise, fire is strong, but water can douse it.

"Water is strong, but clouds can carry it," the rabbi continued. "Clouds are strong but the wind blows them about. The wind can be fierce, but the body can withstand it.

"The body is strong but fear can subdue it. Fear is strong, but wine devours it. Wine is strong, but sleep overtakes it.

"And the ultimate sleep is death, which is the most powerful," Rabbi Judah told the students. "But charitable acts of goodness can deliver us even from death."

[TALMUDIC SOURCE: *Baba Batra 10a*]

Rabbi's Comment:

The rabbis often devised riddles or word games to teach important lessons. In this parable, Rabbi Judah illustrates the progression of commonly known elements of strength, and he concludes that the strongest force among them is an act of sheer goodness. No natural or manmade element can compare to the overwhelming power of the human spirit. When this spirit is engaged in goodness, it can withstand even the strongest force: the power of the grave.

While death has been described as the power to conquer all, it cannot subdue good deeds. Good deeds withstand the test of time, robbing death of its ultimate victory: No structure or monument can compare to the human ability to remember goodness, because such deeds are timeless and eternal.

—◦✧◦—

17. Saving the World Entire

For centuries, rabbis have asked the question: "Why was Adam, a single human being, created first rather than along with other humans?"

While the sages have debated this question throughout the ages, the Talmud reasons that God first created only Adam to teach the value of a single human life to all future generations. Anyone who destroys even one life, destroys an entire world. And he who preserves a single human life has saved the equivalent of the entire world.

In addition, Adam's isolated creation will remind the rest of humanity through the end of time that we all spring from the same parent. Hence, for the sake of peace among humankind, no one can ever say to another, "My father was greater than your father."

The Talmud contrasts the creation of humanity to the minting of coins. No matter how many coins are cast from the same mold, each coin is identical. Even though the Almighty made human beings from a single person, none of us is exactly like any other.

With this awareness, each individual can claim, as Adam did, "The world was created for my sake and my sake alone." For this, each of us must feel richly blessed.

[TALMUDIC SOURCE: *Sanhedrin 37a-b*]

Rabbi's Comment:

The most basic lesson the Talmud teaches is that every human life is sacred. It is also the lesson most frequently overlooked. This parable reminds us of the obligation to behave respectfully toward each person and to consider his or her life as precious as our own. No two individuals are ever identical, so each is a whole and unique creation, with individual attributes, merits, and potential.

INSIGHT

———⧽⧽⧼⧼———

18. The "Dead" Lizard at the Banquet

An apparently dead lizard was discovered in the slaughterhouse at the palace of King Agrippa I. Hence, the slaughterhouse was declared unclean and a long-awaited banquet was canceled. Disappointed, everyone sought the king for his counsel.

"Do not ask me," he said, "go see the queen."

When they asked the queen what to do, she replied, "Do not ask me. Go see the great sage, Rabban Gamaliel."

Upon approaching Gamaliel, he asked, "Is the slaughterhouse hot or cold?"

"It is hot."

"Good," he said. "If this is the case, pour a carafe of cold water on the lizard, and see what happens."

The people rushed back to the slaughterhouse and poured cold water on the lizard. It moved slightly, and then some more. Then it crawled away. The people cheered, and Gamaliel declared that the entire slaughterhouse was clean and proper. "The feast shall commence," he announced, and the people rejoiced.

The king was dependent on the queen, and she upon Gamaliel. Gamaliel, however, relied on his common sense.

[Talmudic source: *Pesachim 88b*]

Rabbi's Comment:

Often careful observance of the simple and the obvious provides solutions to seemingly complicated problems. In this whimsical parable, Gamaliel's application of common sense saved the day. The story proves, once again, that no problem is too great or too trivial for the rabbinic mind to consider.

19. The Old Man and the Fig Tree

When a great emperor's caravan passed by a field in the countryside, the emperor was amused to see a very old man digging a hole in the ground to plant a fig tree.

The emperor ordered the caravan to stop and summoned the old man to come to him. "Old man, why are you working so hard to plant that tree? Surely, you realize that at your age you are unlikely to benefit from your effort by eating the fruit from the tree."

The old man smiled and answered wisely, "If God wishes me to taste the fruit, I will. And if not, my work will not be in vain, for my children will reap its fruit."

Several years went by, and once again the emperor and his caravan passed by the old man's field. The emperor was surprised to see the old man still there. When the old man saw the emperor, he presented to his ruler a basket filled with figs. The farmer reminded the emperor that he was the same old man who was planting a fig tree when the caravan passed by there some time ago. "I would be honored, Your Majesty, if you would accept some figs from the tree that is now in full bloom."

The emperor was so pleased that he commanded his servants to fill the old man's basket with gold.

A neighbor's wife observed the encounter from her field and she ran home to tell her husband.

"Quick," she screamed, "fill a basket with figs and present it to the emperor. It appears that he loves the produce of this region so much that he is willing to reward its farmers with baskets of gold."

The husband did what she told him and took his basket of figs to the emperor, hoping to receive a basket of gold in return. Instead the emperor was so angry with the man's impudence, he ordered his courtiers to throw the figs at the man. Swollen and bruised, the man returned to his wife and reported to her, "I am very lucky to have survived. Had I brought a basket filled with figs, grapes, dates, and apples to the emperor instead of only figs, I would have been killed by my own fruit."

[TALMUDIC SOURCE: *Vayikrah Rabbah 25*]

Rabbi's Comment:

Though we may not see the fruits of our own labors, we must work hard to assure that the next generation will benefit from them. Just as our parents have planted and prepared for us, so must we do the same for our children.

There is still another lesson to learn from this parable. A lazy person consumed by greed does not recognize that hard work itself is the reward, not material compensation. Consequently, when a greedy person attempts a shortcut, to get something for nothing, he or she is bound to be disappointed.

20. Word Games

A group of rabbis were discussing linguistic skills one day when someone remarked that Rabbi Joshua was indeed a master with words. "As far as I'm concerned, Rabbi Joshua, you have no equal," his colleague said.

"Not true," replied Rabbi Joshua.

"But who has ever gotten the best of you?" the rabbi asked. "I can think of nobody."

"At least three people immediately come to mind," Rabbi Joshua said. "Let's see now, I remember a woman who operated an inn, a little girl, and still another time, a little boy."

The other rabbis looked at their colleague in disbelief. "Tell us the details," they asked in unison.

"I once stopped at an inn where the hostess served me a dish of beans," Rabbi Joshua recalled. "I was hungry and I eagerly cleaned my plate. The next day, I was served the same meal, and again, I left nothing on my plate.

"On the third day, however, the hostess had apparently poured excessive salt on the beans, because after one mouthful, I could eat no more.

" 'Why are you not eating?' she asked.

" 'Er—I ate earlier in the day, and I have no appetite,' I answered.

" 'But if that is the case,' she reasoned, 'why did you eat all the bread that was on the table?'

" 'I understand what you have done,' she continued before I could reply. 'It is what I would expect from a fine man like you. You left today's dish as a reward to the server for having served you the previous two days. Yes, Rabbi, you followed the table etiquette that our sages have taught us. A satisfied guest leaves something for the server to enjoy afterward.'

" 'You are correct,' I said. 'I left the beans for the waiter to enjoy.' "

The other rabbis shook their heads in awe. "Now tell us about the little girl."

"Once while I was traveling along the road, I observed a path through a field. I was tired and knew that I could save some time and energy by taking the shortcut. As I began walking through the field, a little girl called to me. 'Excuse me, sir, but you are trespassing through private property.'

" 'But I'm not walking upon the actual field,' I defended myself. 'You see, my child, I am trudging on this pathway that cuts through the field. Do you understand the difference?'

" 'Yes, there is a path upon which you travel,' the little girl said. 'But it was formed by illegal trespassers like yourself.' "

Again the other rabbis were dumbfounded to think that a little girl was able to get the best of Rabbi Joshua. "Now tell us about the little boy," they urged.

"On another trip, I approached a little boy sitting at a crossroads. 'Tell me, young boy, which road should I take to get to the city?'

" 'This road to the right is short, but it is long,' the boy replied. And with another riddle, he said, 'However, this road to the left is long, but it is short.'

"Choosing a shorter journey, I embarked on the road to the right. After a while, although I was able to see the city in the distance, the road was so obstructed by gardens and orchards that I could not proceed. So I reversed my direction and once again came across the little boy where I had first met him.

" 'Didn't you say this road was shorter?' I asked.

" 'Did I tell you it was also longer?' he answered.

"I smiled and kissed him on the forehead. 'Oh, the people of

Israel must be smiling happily today,' I said, 'to have such a wise young person among them.' "

[TALMUDIC SOURCE: *Eruvin 53b*]

Rabbi's Comment:

Word games and riddles were popular during Talmudic discourse. The greatest rabbis took particular delight in challenging their students, often demonstrating a lesson by laughing at themselves. It was a sign of humility for a scholarly rabbi to portray himself in a story that ended with egg on his face.

In this parable, Rabbi Joshua wisely wanted his peers to recognize that nobody, not even he, knows everything. And under certain circumstances, it was possible that even a small child could outwit a learned scholar. This parable of the highly respected Rabbi Joshua showed that lessons can be learned from all people, regardless of occupation, gender, or age. It's a lesson we should all remember.

21. The Doubting Fisherman

A man sitting across from his rabbi lamented, "I am so un-learned! I feel unworthy when I am around educated people."

"Why do you feel this way?" the rabbi asked.

"I know very little." Stumbling for words, he sighed. "In fact, I have no idea what is contained in the Torah."

The rabbi sat back in deep thought. Carefully choosing his words, he inquired, "If you feel this way, why didn't you spend some time in study? Even if you can't read, certainly you could have sat with the sages and acquired wisdom from their teachings."

"What would be the use?" the man replied. "God did not give me the capacity for understanding and discernment."

"What is your occupation?" the rabbi asked.

"I am just a fisherman," he meekly answered.

"A fisherman!" the rabbi exclaimed. "Well then, who taught you to weave nets? And where did you learn how to cast them over the waters in order to catch fish?"

"Oh, I suppose this was a gift that I acquired from Heaven. Yes, I do have the understanding to master this single skill. This is my one successful purpose."

The wise rabbi said, "Do you not suppose that if God has given you the acumen to earn a good living as a fisherman, you were also given sufficient intelligence to learn Torah? After all, it is said in the Torah, 'These laws are not hard for you. They are not distant but very near.' This is found in the book of Deuteronomy."

As the fisherman listened intently, he began to weep. "Yes, Rabbi, you are right. If I was able to learn to fish, I can also catch a few words of Torah."

"Do not be dismayed," the rabbi said in a soft voice. "Other people have thought like you. But it does not matter what a man's occupation is. As long as you are willing to learn something new each day, it is never too late to educate yourself."

[TALMUDIC SOURCE: *Sedar Eliyahu Zuta 14*]

Rabbi's Comment:

The Talmud teaches us that the learning which we began at an early age must continue throughout our lives. And not only do we learn new lessons daily for the sake of our own growth and development, but because our acquired wisdom will, in turn, benefit others. The well-being of a community is based upon the willingness of its people to engage in study and to provide opportunities for knowledge and growth for people of all ages. This lesson teaches the importance of understanding that everyone has the capacity to learn the Torah on some level. What each individual brings to the study of the text is not only a particular intellect and experience, but a willingness to grow spiritually throughout a lifetime. It is never too late to gain insight, and we should never be intimidated by others. Neither should we underestimate our capacity to learn something new each day.

22. *Real Jewels*

Rabbi Hiyyah bar Abba and Rabbi Abbahu were hailed as two of the greatest rabbinic scholars of their time. By sheer coincidence, they both appeared in the same village to speak on the same day. Each attracted a sizable audience.

Rabbi Hiyyah lectured on serious matters of legal concern, while Rabbi Abbahu's teachings were filled with stories and parables. It wasn't long before all the people who had gathered to hear Rabbi Hiyyah had drifted into the growing crowd assembled to hear Rabbi Abbahu's wonderful tales.

Understandably, Hiyyah was upset as he found himself with only a few listeners. Later that day he said to Abbahu, "I have a story to tell you. Once two merchants came to a village to sell their wares. One sold precious stones and the other sold cheap trinkets. At first, all the villagers circled around the merchant with the expensive goods. Naturally, they were curious to see his fine gems. But when it came time to actually make a purchase, they flocked to the merchant with the trinkets, and that's where they spent their money."

[TALMUDIC SOURCE: *Sotah 40a*]

Rabbi's Comment:

Human nature prompts us to desire the most ostensibly valuable items, but to most, they are unattainable. Since we are unable to acquire all that we crave, we often settle for what we feel we can afford. In this parable, Rabbi Hiyyah's discourse required considerably more scholarship than did Rabbi Abbahu's easily accessible stories and parables. It is no wonder that the jewels of instruction from Rabbi Hiyyah were discarded; after all, with the exception of a select few listeners, his words were beyond the comprehension of the masses. No matter how difficult it may be to comprehend an original idea, each individual should continue to seek real knowledge and insight, and always retain the awareness that the value of true wisdom exceeds material possessions.

23. The Emperor's Daughter and the Ugly Scholar

The daughter of a powerful emperor was introduced to Rabbi Joshua, one of his generation's great scholars. While the rabbi was noted for his immense intellect, he was not considered an attractive man.

The emperor's daughter, not known for her finesse, took one look at him and remarked, "Oh my! Why does such glorious and wonderful wisdom have to come in such an ugly container?"

Fortunately, Rabbi Joshua was a patient and wise man. Rather than taking offense at her insult, he asked her, "Why does your father store his wine in an earthen pitcher?"

"But, Rabbi, that is the way wine has always been stored," she replied.

"Certainly people of your family's exalted station could afford to keep their wine in vessels of a more precious material, such as gold or silver," the rabbi said.

Later that day, the young woman told her father what the scholarly rabbi had said. She then persuaded him to send his servants to the cellar to transfer all of the wine stored in earthen containers to beautiful jewel-encrusted gold and silver mugs. It was only a matter of time before the emperor's wine reacted to the containers' metal and turned sour.

The disgruntled emperor summoned the rabbi to his palace. "Why did you give my daughter such poor counsel?" he demanded. "Surely you knew what would happen to my wine!"

"Yes," Rabbi Joshua answered. "But I did it to demonstrate to your daughter that wisdom and knowledge, like fine wine, is kept best in the plainest vessel."

The emperor thanked the rabbi for teaching his daughter a valuable lesson. His daughter asked, "Rabbi Joshua, does this mean there are no handsome scholars amongst you?"

"Of course there are," the rabbi responded. "But just think how much more their scholarship would be appreciated if people were not distracted by their handsome appearance!"

[Talmudic source: *Ta'anit 7a*]

Rabbi's Comment:

The emperor's young daughter learned that greater understanding often lies beneath the surface, and sometimes, one must dig for it. This parable reminds us that we should not assess the contents of a container (person) by its outward appearance, or as we say today, judge a book by its cover. Neither should we be negatively influenced by our first impression of someone without learning more about him.

FULFILLMENT

———◦◦◦◦———

24. In Pursuit of Scholarship and Riches

Ilfa and Yochanan were study partners of the Torah, dedicated to learning the application of the law. Unfortunately, their studies consumed so much time that they were unable to meet their financial obligations. To overcome their indigence, the two scholars decided to launch a business career.

Traveling to a nearby village in search of business, they stopped to rest by a wall of ruins. Two ministering angels observed them and commented on their enterprise. They were so close that Rabbi Yochanan could hear their conversation.

"Why don't we knock over this wall," one angel said to the other, "and kill these two unworthy men. They deserve to die for their sins; they have deserted their studies to seek profit in commerce."

"Let them be," the second angel replied. "No matter what you think, I believe one of them still has much to accomplish and deserves mercy."

Shocked by the angels' remarks, Yochanan said to his traveling companion, "Did you hear what I just heard?"

"I heard nothing," Ilfa answered.

Yochanan thought: Since it was I who heard and not Ilfa, I am evidently the one who has yet so much to accomplish.

"I have decided to turn back," Yochanan said, "and resume my studies. Let it be known, my friend, that because of me, if for no other reason, there will always be poverty in the land."

So Rabbi Yochanan continued with his studies while Ilfa pursued a business career. Many years later, Ilfa visited the village where once he studied Torah. Rabbi Yochanan had become the head of the school.

The scholars said to him, "Perhaps if you had remained, Ilfa, you, instead of Rabbi Yochanan, would be the master of the school."

This comment disturbed Ilfa so much that he climbed aboard a ship and stood at the top of its mast. He proclaimed, "If anyone questions me about the teachings of either Rabbi Hiyya or Rabbi Hoshiah, and I am unable to answer correctly, I will drown myself."

An old man stepped forward with a very difficult question on inheritance law. Without hesitation, Ilfa responded brilliantly. His explanation was so astute and proper, his scholarship was admired by all.

[TALMUDIC SOURCE: *Ta'anit 20b*]

Rabbi's Comment:

Although Ilfa spent many years in business pursuits, he proved that he had maintained and even expanded his knowledge of the law. Thus, this parable teaches us that while a life of learning and intellectual growth may be enticing, reality presents us with the need to make a living. Spending all our waking hours learning for the sake of learning is not an option available to most people. Still, it is possible to be fiscally responsible and pursue knowledge; God created within us the capacity to both attain financial rewards and fulfill our intellectual needs.

25. *It's Always Something*

Rabbi Mani was troubled by his wealthy in-laws. "My father-in-law's family really bothers me," he complained to his teacher, Rabbi Isaac ben Eliashav.

"I will offer a prayer," Rabbi Isaac said, "that they will become poor."

And incredibly, this is precisely what happened. All of Rabbi Mani's in-laws lost their riches.

Sometime later, Rabbi Mani confided again to Rabbi Isaac that his wife's relatives continued to annoy him. "Now, they are so poor that they constantly pester me for money."

"Okay," his teacher said, "I will offer a prayer that your in-laws become rich again." And, lo and behold, their riches were restored.

Again Rabbi Mani complained to his mentor, "I can no longer tolerate my wife Hannah's homeliness." Rabbi Isaac prayed, "May Hannah become beautiful."

Rabbi Mani returned to his home and found his wife ravishing. But even this failed to satisfy him, because she had also become bossy. Once more, he begged his teacher to intercede, for his wife was now ordering him around.

Finally, Rabbi Isaac said to his student, "Once and for all, I will offer a prayer, May Hannah become ugly again."

When Rabbi Mani returned home, his wife had become ugly again. This time, he recognized how foolish he had been, and at last, he was content.

[TALMUDIC SOURCE: *Ta'anit 23b*]

Rabbi's Comment:

We often do not know what we want out of life. Likewise, we occasionally do not recognize the treasures or the blessings we actually possess. And even when we have that awareness, we do not always appreciate it. This parable simply teaches us to avoid greed and be grateful for what we have; in particular, we should appreciate ourselves, our mate, and our family. However, when we are content, we must strive for improvement. We should stretch to extend our limits and exercise our creativity.

Life is a journey, and the truly contented person finds satisfaction at every step of the way. In the contemporary world, this is an elusive virtue, but not an unattainable one.

26. The King and Eye

While traveling homeward to Macedonia, Alexander stopped by a stream of sweet water and unpacked his meal of salted fish. Upon washing the fish in the stream, its taste became sweet and fragrant. He then decided to refresh himself with the water and hiked upstream to its spring. According to legend, Alexander arrived at the gateway to the Garden of Eden.

"Open this gate," he ordered.

"This is the Lord's gateway, and only the righteous are permitted to enter," answered a voice from above.

"I am a king," Alexander said. "I am worthy enough to receive something. Do not send me away empty-handed."

So Alexander was given a human eyeball, which he carried back to Greece. Thinking that the eyeball must be valuable, he placed it on a scale to be weighed against gold and silver. But no matter how much precious metal was brought, he was unable to pile up enough riches to outweigh the eye. Alarmed, Alexander summoned the rabbis and asked them to interpret this mystery. The rabbis explained to the great leader that since this was a human eye, it desired everything it saw, and no amount of wealth could balance the lust it represented.

"How can this be?" Alexander challenged them.

"Scoop up some dust and cover the eye with it," the scholars suggested.

Alexander covered the eye, and immediately the scale tipped to the other side. Once blinded, the eye's desire for greed abates.

"When it comes to human greed," the rabbis said, "the eye is never satisfied."

[TALMUDIC SOURCE: *Tamid 32b*]

Rabbi's Comment:

The human eye is a metaphor for human desire. It is never satisfied until it is closed forever at death, and this, the rabbis teach, is the tragic flaw in so many of us. Human greed and the need for ever-expanding wealth and power have spelled the downfall of many an empire. Alexander the Great and the Greek Empire were no exceptions. The artifacts and ancient ruins of Greek civilization tell of their once-great past, but their greed in wishing to conquer the world led to their destruction. Thus, the Talmud teaches that true life and length of days can be found not in insatiable desire but in the realization that we can be satisfied with our portion. Being pleased with what one has is the only road to fulfillment, and fulfillment is the only means to true and eternal peace.

27. The Inner Voice

During the months of April, May, and early June, Israel always enjoyed the bounty of its barley harvest. The gathering of the grain, when farmers worked in the fields under the warming skies, was an annual ritual. One of the most arduous tasks was the grinding. The men labored all day long. Eventually, they were able to transform the barley corn into fine flour. They repeatedly ground the barley to the finest flour possible, until it was pure enough to be considered for an offering at the Temple in Jerusalem. The grinding process was over only when the flour was as fine as it could possibly be.

At first a grinder might think it is impossible to produce a finer flour. Again and again, when the grinder thought he had reached the point where no improvement was possible, the rabbis teach that the grinder relied on a voice. And what would the voice always say? Nothing less than, "Keep grinding." For the grinder needed this voice, and the voice kept the grinder on track. "Keep grinding, keep improving. Keep refining the flour until it is as smooth as it can be."

[TALMUDIC SOURCE: *The Midrash*]

Rabbi's Comment:

What applies to the harvest of barley applies to the harvest of life. Just as we reach a point in our work where we believe no further effort is required, we, too, need a voice from within to say, "Keep grinding. Keep improving. Keep working and refining and polishing to improve life to do even better."

As long as we are able to reap the harvest, further improvement is always possible. And, in this effort, there is no end. Further improvement is always attainable because perfection is never achieved.

The voice gently whispers in our ears at moments of despair, at times when we think we have done enough, and when we are frustrated with the belief that we can do no more. The voice repeats, "Keep grinding."

Our work is never finished because we are not required to complete the task. Neither are we free from the need to continue our work in our constant struggle to live.

28. The Rabbi and the Harlot

Rabbi Eliezer ben Dordia had the dubious distinction of having visited every harlot in the world. So when he heard about a beautiful woman for hire on the coast, he was compelled to visit her. And although she charged a full purse for her services, the rabbi left the hill country and traveled the long journey, which included crossing seven rivers, to be with her.

During his visit, the harlot blew out a puff of air and said, "As this breath will never again return to its place of origin, you, Eliezer ben Dordia, shall never receive repentance from the Almighty."

Her remark upset him so he fled back to the hill country. Stopping between two high mountains, he knelt to pray.

Ben Dordia called out, "O ye mountains and great heights, pray for mercy on my behalf!"

The mountains rumbled, "Until we, who also are in need, are granted mercy ourselves, how can we request it for you? For we know from the prophet Isaiah, that 'The mountains shall depart, and the hills be removed.' "

The rabbi then cried to the heavens and the earth, "Will you plead mercy for me?"

They too, responded, "Until we who are in need are granted mercy, how can we ask for you? The prophet Isaiah has said, 'For the heavens shall vanish like smoke, and the earth shall wear out and fray like a garment.' "

So the rabbi appealed to the sun and the moon, who responded similarly.

"How can we, in need of mercy, help you? Isaiah also declared, 'The moon shall be confounded and the sun ashamed.' "

In desperation, ben Dordia begged the stars and constellations, "Plead mercy for me."

But they too answered out of their own need for mercy. " 'The hosts of Heaven shall all turn to vapor and ash, and disintegrate away.' "

Suddenly, the rabbi understood his predicament, and said aloud, "The matter seems to lie solely with me. If I am to gain mercy, I must ask for myself."

With his head between his knees, Rabbi Eliezer ben Dordia wept aloud and repented until his soul ascended to Heaven. A Heavenly voice echoed through the mountains, proclaiming forgiveness and eternal reward for Rabbi Eliezer ben Dordia.

And even though ben Dordia was exonerated from his great sin, he died. The explanation was that because Rabbi Eliezer ben Dordia was so addicted to immorality, departing this life was the only means to attain forgiveness.

[TALMUDIC SOURCE: *Avodah Zarah 17*a]

Rabbi's Comment:

The harlot's harsh remark prompted Rabbi Eliezer ben Dordia to reconsider his behavior and seek forgiveness. Realizing his iniquities, the rabbi felt unworthy of asking mercy from God on his own. So he sought the help of Creation. However, the hills and mountains, the sun and the moon, the stars, and the vast array of the universe were unable to assist. Ultimately, the rabbi concluded that forgiveness was available only if he sought it himself with all his heart and soul. Here, we learn that true repentance exists within each of us, if we are willing to change deep within ourselves. Hence, there is no stronger petition for God's mercy than that of the human heart. With this power, anything, even absolution by God, is possible.

Interestingly, the Talmud does not censure its personalities. In this respect, it describes the transgressions of the rabbis and sages, noting that we are all human, subject to impulses that have been the joy and the bane of mankind since Creation. Along with the goodness in each of us, there is a tendency for evil, and both vie for our attention.

29. Steel on Steel

When Rabbi Hama pondered aloud the saying, "Steel sharpens steel," his colleagues immediately began a discussion relating steel to learning.

"Just as a blade is sharpened by contact with another blade," one rabbi said, "so do two students sharpen each other's intellect when they study law together."

"Aha!" said Rabbi Ashi. "I agree. And I think a student of the law must also be hard as steel, or he is no scholar."

"Practically speaking, you are correct," replied Rabbi Abba. "To break down difficult issues into simpler ones requires a scholar, as a hammer must be able to break a rock into many pebbles."

"Nevertheless, a man must learn to be gentle," insisted Rabbina. "After all, he should never harbor animosity or contempt in his heart."

"But what if a student finds his studies to be as hard as steel?" added Resh Lakish. He continued with an answer, "It is because he was unable to organize his studies properly. Let him attend classes even more regularly and diligently, and gain greater strength."

"If a student encounters such difficulty learning," Raba interjected, "it must be because his teacher is unsympathetic to him and discouraging. In my opinion, he should turn to his fellow students, who will address the problem on his behalf with his teacher. His teacher then can encourage and praise his efforts and edify him.

"One also strengthens steel in this way: one must work it, and coax the edge onto the blade," Raba concluded. "All we have discussed is true, but we must also remember that a blade used in anger can only bring destruction. Such is the case when two scholars, living in the same village, constantly disagree. By their intolerance they will lose their edge through anger. In addition, they will anger others."

[TALMUDIC SOURCE: *Ta'anit 7a–8a*]

Rabbi's Comment:

The rabbis used the metaphor of a steel blade to symbolize the importance of studying or learning in pairs. This has been the long tradition in the pattern of rabbinic learning. A single blade becomes dull through prolonged usage; against another sharpened blade it can test its strength. Two blades hone each other through use, one against the other.

Still, while the rabbis concurred that the metaphor of steel is applicable to the growth and development of a scholar, yet another dimension must be considered. As steel is tempered, we too must be tempered to display gentleness, kindness, and tolerance to all. The discipline of study also teaches us to avoid harboring animosity or contempt, and guides us in turning away from the words or deeds that might antagonize others. To deny the added effects of scholarly endeavor is tantamount to purposely dulling the blade of wisdom and truth.

30. The Joy of Sabbath

Rabbi Joshua ben Hanania had befriended the powerful Roman Caesar Hadrian; the two men met regularly to discuss and debate the issues of the day.

During one particular conversation, the emperor asked his companion, "Why does the dish you serve on the Sabbath have such a pleasing aroma?"

"It is because we Jews have a unique spice which is called *shabbat'* [the Sabbath]," the rabbi answered. "We put the seasoning into the dish, and from it our food gets its delicious aroma."

"Give me some of that special spice," Hadrian commanded.

With a warm smile, Rabbi Hanania replied, "It is with regret, O Caesar, that I must inform you this spice works its special effect only on those who observe the Sabbath. But to those who do not keep the day of rest, the spice has no effect at all."

[TALMUDIC SOURCE: *Shabbat 119a*]

Rabbi's Comment:

How sweet is the Sabbath day to all who prepare for it, anticipate its arrival, and enjoy its soothing refreshment. For these people, no other day can compare. It is particularly special to the regular observer who relishes the Sabbath's simple requirements. The Sabbath is a day when no work is done and no effort toward worldly gain is pursued. It sanctions a time for the body and mind to relax and rejuvenate. This is the therapeutic message contained in the sweet aroma of the Sabbath.

By pausing on this one day of the week from our daily routine of working, creating, earning and spending our wages, we can heighten our appreciation for the satisfaction of success, and at the same time, savor the sweet fragrance of relaxation and refreshment.

DESTINY

—⟨⟩—

31. The Rains Came

While Rabbi Hanina ben Dosa was traveling between villages, a strong storm drenched him. In frustration, he held his arms to the sky and protested, "Master of the Universe, all the world is at rest, but I, Hanina ben Dosa, am in turmoil."

No sooner than he had spoken, the rains passed.

Upon arriving home from his trip, the rabbi raised his arms to the sky and said, "Master of the Universe, all the world is in turmoil, but I, Hanina ben Dosa, am at rest."

The rains began again.

One rabbi asked, "What do the prayers of Hanina ben Dosa teach us?" Another answered by explaining that prayers offered by a traveler take precedence over the prayers of even pious and powerful priests.

[TALMUDIC SOURCE: *Ta'anit 24b*]

Rabbi's Comment:

A person's journey through life is often unstable, insecure, and stressful. Here, the Talmudic metaphor of a man traveling through storms reminds us that the gates of prayer are open wide to those who suffer the distress of living with doubt and trepidation. The prayers of the secure and powerful may often be heeded, but not before God tries to ease the worried hearts of those who have not reached their destinations, both geographical and spiritual.

32. The Death of the Great Sages

After the Temple's destruction, the disciples assembled in sadness. They grieved the loss of their great teachers, noting that each sage's departure created a monumental void.

When Rabbi Mier died, the disciples stopped composing fables. Ben Azzai, said to have been married to the Torah, carried to his grave the diligence of study. And explanation of the Torah vanished with the passing of ben Zoma, the greatest expositor. With Rabbi Joshua's death, goodness perished. Rabbi Simeon ben Gamliel's death brought locusts and troubles multiplied. And the passing of Eliezer ben Azaria obliterated the sages' wealth.

Akiba extracted new ideas from every letter and every nuance of the Torah; with his death the glory of the Torah was lost. Loving kindness disintegrated after the death of Rabbi Hanina ben Dosa. Rabbi Jose Ketanta, the youngest sage of piety, left none of that quality behind.

Known as the lamp of Israel, Rabbi Yochanan ben Zakkai died along with the luster of wisdom. Upon Rabban Gamliel the elder's death, purity disappeared. Rabbi Ishmael ben Fabi, appointed high priest by Agrippa, took with him the luster of the priesthood. And gone was humility and the fear of sin when Rabbi Judah HaNasi died.

Rabbi Phineas ben Yair lamented, "When the second Temple was destroyed, scholars and wise men covered their heads in shame. Men known for their good deeds were disregarded, and insensitive demagogues grew powerful. No one was left to care for Israel's well-being; now no one prays on Israel's behalf, or asks about his neighbor."

"Upon whom shall we rely if not on God in Heaven?" mourned the disciples.

Rabbi Eliezer said, "Since the Temple's destruction, sages became like schoolteachers; schoolteachers like synagogue attendants; synagogue attendants like the masses; and the masses become more and more debased. No one was left to pray and ask, 'On whom should we rely if not upon God in Heaven?'

"As the Messiah approaches," Eliezer continued, "rudeness will thrive and honor diminish; drunkenness will increase; the government will be corrupted, and no one will challenge it. The gathering places of scholars will be disgraced. The lower Galilee will be destroyed; the upper Galilee will be left desolate. Beggars will wander from place to place without pity. The wisdom of the scribes will fade.

"Those who fear sin will be despised. Truth will be impotent. Youths will shame old men; the young will sit while the old ones stand. Sons will revile their fathers, daughters will insult their mothers; enemies will arise from a man's own household. The face of the generation will be like that of a dog! So upon whom shall we rely if not upon God in Heaven?"

"Yet there is hope," taught Rabbi Phineas. "There is hope if we remember that mindfulness leads to cleanliness; cleanliness leads to purity; purity to abstinence; abstinence to holiness; holiness to the possession of the Holy Spirit; and the Holy Spirit to the end of time, which is heralded by the coming of Elijah, the prophet of blessed memory. Amen."

[TALMUDIC SOURCE: *Sotah 49a*]

—◦◦◦—

Rabbi's Comment:

Each of the great rabbis mentioned possessed a notable trait that elevated him above his peers. Together, the collective loss of these great minds was devastating to an entire generation of students and disciples. These sages were the ultimate role models of their time; they were the intellectual and moral leaders, representing all that was good and righteous.

During the first century of the Common Era, Jerusalem's destruction and Israel's conquest wreaked havoc within the Jewish community, creating political, moral, and intellectual disarray. And yet, in spite of their loss, the Jews retained their hope and faith in God, believing they would survive and new leaders would appear.

This parable ends with hope offered by Rabbi Phineas that the rabbis' values and morals will live on. Even amid enormous anguish, the community must not despair; new scholars and sages will arise, and create and maintain new standards, raising everyone to new heights. So while the sages may be gone, their precious legacy has endured throughout the ages. Perhaps it was no more evident than in the twentieth century in today's post-Holocaust world. With the loss of countless brilliant teachers and students in Europe, many survivors feared that their scholarship would never be replaced. But since the end of World War II, exceptional efforts have been invested by Jewish communities around the world to develop new and even greater houses of study. Consequently, there is hope that the level of learning may someday equal or even surpass the greatness that existed prior to the devastation of European Jewry.

33. A Fish Out of Water

Many centuries ago, the land of Israel was under siege by a sovereign power that had forbidden Jews from studying their sacred texts. In defiance of this ordinance, Rabbi Akiba conducted classes openly in public areas.

"Why do you take such a risk?" he was asked. "Surely you must be aware of the punishment you could receive."

In reply, Akiba told this story: A fox took his morning stroll along the river, looked into the water and noticed a school of fish darting to and fro. The curious fox asked one of the fish, "Why do you swim as if you are frightened?"

"To avoid being caught in the nets of the people who are always trying to catch us," one fish answered.

"Then why don't you come out of the water," the fox suggested, "and we can live together in peace."

"Aren't you the one who is referred to as the most cunning of all creatures?" the fish responded.

"Indeed, you are correct," bragged the fox.

"Well, I don't think you are clever at all," said the fish, "because your suggestion is ridiculous."

"Ridiculous?" the fox exclaimed.

"Yes," replied the fish. "If we have reason to fear for our lives in water, which is our natural environment, imagine the fear we'd have on land in an unnatural environment."

The fox listened as the fish continued: "Being fish, our survival depends on the water."

[TALMUDIC SOURCE: *Berachot 61b*]

Rabbi's Comment:

Rabbi Akiba's timeless lesson teaches that just as fish would die out of water, the Jewish people would cease to exist without their natural environment of sacred text study. When Akiba was alive, the Romans attempted to eradicate the Jews by forbidding them to study Torah, which was the single most unifying bond between them. Here, the great sage offers insight into how protective Jews must be in order to preserve their tradition and maintain their "habitat" and identity. Cunning forces, as the one exemplified by the fox, may try to undermine it through deception, but the awareness of this effort can help the Jews survive, but only in the place where they belong.

SECTION II

———⟊⟊⟊———

Living as a Community

The following parables focus on how people should relate to one another as a community. The Talmud was written at a time when the Jewish community centered around the guidance of the rabbis, who served as revered teachers and leaders; their responsibility was to teach people how to live in harmony.

The family always represented the nucleus of the community, so several parables in this section discuss the relationships between spouses as well as parents and their offspring. They contain insightful teachings on what the rabbinic leaders believed were the right ways to interact with friends, neighbors, and strangers.

RESPECT
34. Hidden Pearls
35. The Greatest Blessing
36. The Dedicated Wife
37. Honor Thy Wife
38. Adam's Rib
39. Matchmaker, Matchmaker
40. Sour Grapes
41. The True Heir
42. The Deep Sleep
43. True Inheritance
44. Partners in Creation

HUMILITY
45. The Appreciative Guest
46. Honor Is Not an Option
47. The Sting of Criticism
48. Kamsa and Bar Kamsa
49. Wisdom Is Mightier Than the Sword

COMPASSION
50. The Price of Hesitation
51. A Person of Character
52. Food for Thought
53. The Measure of a Mensch
54. The Ambiguity of Tradition
55. The Rowdy Neighbors
56. Sharp Words
57. The Visit
58. The Hillel-Shammai Debate
59. The Dream of Wine

HARMONY
60. The People's Choice
61. People Need People
62. Healing Hands
63. Four Types of Students
64. The Miraculous Human Body
65. Twice Cured
66. The Captives
67. Extreme Patience
68. The Virtue of Silence
69. The Siege of Jerusalem
70. Sunrise, Sunset

FAIRNESS
71. Enough Is Not Enough
72. The Sale of a Ship
73. Twelve Wells
74. The Letter and the Spirit
75. The Buried Purse of Gold
76. The Oath
77. The Scale of Justice
78. Bitter Wine
79. Alexander the Not-So-Great

RESPECT

━━◈◈◈◈━━

34. Hidden Pearls

Rabbi Yochanan and Rabbi Eliezer, students of Rabbi Joshua, dropped in on their teacher.

"What new insights did you learn in the study house today?" Joshua inquired.

The students met his query with blank expressions.

"It is impossible to attend a class session," Joshua prompted, "without learning something new. Whose honor was it to speak this Sabbath and what did he say?"

"Rabbi Eliezer ben Azaria spoke on the giving of the Torah," one answered. "He discussed how Moses was instructed to assemble the people—the men, women and children—to receive the Torah at Sinai."

"Good," said Rabbi Joshua. "And what was Rabbi Eliezer's interpretation?"

"It was insightful," the other replied. "The men came to learn and the women came to listen. Then Rabbi Eliezer asked, 'But why did Moses bring the children?' And he then answered his own question."

"And what purpose did he give?" Joshua asked.

"The little ones came so that those adults who brought them could merit further reward," chimed Yochanan and Eliezer.

Rabbi Joshua smiled. "Here you have a beautiful pearl, and you chose to hide it from me. How could you do such a thing?"

[TALMUDIC SOURCE: *Chagigah 3a*]

───◈◈◈───

Rabbi's Comment:

Two meaningful messages spring from this parable. First, the rabbis wished to remind all who study never to become so proud that they miss the lessons that come from human interaction. We must be aware that no matter how educated an individual may be, he or she can always learn an important lesson simply by being with others. Therefore, it is wrong, even arrogant, to believe you cannot learn from another person even if that person is a child. Rabbi Joshua taught his students to avoid this arrogance by being amenable to learning new and valuable lessons from everyone.

Still another message in this parable is to recognize children as a double reward. By including children when we learn, study, and grow, we enhance our world and theirs as well.

───◈◈◈───

35. The Greatest Blessing

Rabbi Isaac was not only Rabbi Nahman's mentor, but his dear friend. At the end of a long day of study, Rabbi Nahman asked his teacher to give him a blessing before the two men parted.

Rabbi Isaac replied, "Your request reminds me of the story of a man traveling across the desert. Not long after the start of his journey, the man runs out of food and water. Overcome by exhaustion, he can go no further. Fortunately, he comes upon a beautiful tree laden with magnificent fruit. The man eats a few pieces, thinking to himself, 'My, this is the tastiest fruit I have ever eaten.' Observing the tree's strong branches, he notices that they are bountiful with leaves. Under the tree's abundant shade, the man rests peacefully while he is recovering his strength. Upon awakening, he spots a bubbling brook flowing near the tree's roots, and he drinks its cool, refreshing water. Like the fruit, it too is nourishing and delicious.

"Filled with vigor, the man wishes to express his appreciation to the tree before embarking on his journey. 'You have given me so much,' he said. 'How can I bless you in return?'"

Rabbi Isaac turned to his student and asked, "Should the man bless the tree by saying, 'May your fruit be sweet'? But that would be foolish, since he had already enjoyed the sweet taste of its fruit.

"Should the man bless the tree by saying, 'May your limbs be wide and filled with beautiful leaves'? But that would be foolish, since he had already sought refuge from the sun under the shade that the tree had provided.

"Should he have blessed the tree by saying, 'May clean, cool waters flow swiftly beside you to nourish your roots'? But that too would be foolish, since such waters already flowed by the tree."

"How then should the man bless the tree?" asked Rabbi Nahman.

Rabbi Isaac turned to his friend and answered, "He should have asked in blessing that all of the tree's saplings be blessed just as the tree itself was."

With this, the learned rabbi said, "And this is the way it is with you, my dear friend and student. For how can I seek to bless you? With knowledge? That would be foolish because you already have knowledge. With wealth? That would be silly because the riches of the world are already yours.

"Perhaps with children," Rabbi Isaac continued. "I could ask that you be blessed with children, but you already have children.

"And so my most sincere and deep hope for you in blessing is simply this: May your children grow to be as you are, and bless you with the same abundance of goodness that you give to others."

[TALMUDIC SOURCE: *Ta'anit 5b*]

——◦◦◦——

Rabbi's Comment:

We are all blessed with one thing or another; it may be a measure of material goods, or intellect, or physical attributes. Yet, there is no greater blessing than to see whatever goodness we possess reproduced in our off-spring. Another blessing is to see the values that we cherish carried on by those who come after us.

Above all, we want everything with which we have

been blessed to be passed on to our children, so they can continue to offer the same goodness to the world. This is the greatest blessing, and there is no finer legacy.

36. The Dedicated Wife

A wealthy man's daughter fell in love with Akiba, a poor shepherd, and the two were soon married. When her father learned of the marriage, he was so upset that he vowed she would never inherit his wealth.

Unable to afford even a pillow, the poor couple slept on straw placed on the floor of their humble home. Each morning, they would pick straw out of their hair. "If only I were wealthy," Akiba often told his loving wife, "I would give you the gift of a golden Jerusalem."

The prophet Elijah happened to pass near their house one day and appeared at their doorstep. Masquerading as a beggar, he cried out, "Straw! Straw! Please give me some straw to place on the ground, because there is nothing for my wife to lie upon."

The good Akiba said to his wife, "My dear, as you can see, there are some people who are even less fortunate than we. We must give that man some of our straw."

"Akiba, you are so good and so wise," she said, "you should leave home to study and someday become a scholar."

So Akiba left home and went to study with Rabbi Eliezer and Rabbi Joshua. He remained with them for twelve years and then decided to return to his wife. Upon arriving at his home, he stood outside the window and overheard a wicked man saying to his wife, "What a terrible marriage you have. Not only is your husband socially beneath your family, but he has left and now you live alone like a widow!"

Akiba's wife defended him: "If Akiba were here right at this moment, I would say to him, 'Go, my dear husband, and study and learn for another twelve years.' "

With that, Akiba said to himself, "As my wife wishes, I will return to my studies," and he did so for another twelve years.

At the end of that time, twenty-four years had passed and he had not seen his wife. When he returned home this time, however, he came as the renowned, wise, and learned Rabbi Akiba, a great scholar with a following of 24,000 disciples. As he entered the village, it seemed as though the entire world had come out to greet him, and in that crowd was his wife.

The same wicked man stopped her and demanded, "And just where do you think you are going, you poor, ignorant woman?"

"I am going to meet my husband, Rabbi Akiba," she answered. "My husband is a righteous man, and surely he will embrace me with warmth and love."

As she approached, Akiba's disciples attempted to restrain her. However, when the learned rabbi recognized her, he exclaimed to the large crowd, "Let her through! This wonderful woman is my wife, who is my very heart and soul. My scholarship, as well as yours, are all because of her!"

Her father, by now an old man, heard what had occurred and renounced his vow. He wished them much happiness as husband and wife.

[TALMUDIC SOURCE: *Nedarin 50a*]

Rabbi's Comment:

This is a classic tale about Rabbi Akiba, who spent his early years as an uneducated shepherd and studied to become one of the greatest rabbinic scholars of all time through the encouragement and wisdom of his wife.

This parable reminds us of the strong, positive, and inspiring influence a good spouse can have. It also emphasizes the profound influence acquired knowledge can have on an entire community.

Rabbi Akiba is widely quoted throughout rabbinic text, but little is known about his wife. She is clearly entitled to praise and honor for being the force behind his intellect, and it is a pity that her role in Jewish history still remains in the shadow of her great husband.

37. Honor Thy Wife

"One should never publicly put his neighbor to shame," one man told another.

"Even more importantly," his companion answered, "a man must take great care not to upset his wife."

"I agree, but how can a man be so careful to avoid upsetting his wife? For haven't we been taught that a man who takes his wife's advice will end up ruined?" the first man asked.

"But that's absolutely untrue," replied the friend. "Why, even if a man is so tall and his wife is so short that her voice can barely be heard, he must bend down to listen to her, even if she whispers."

Rabbi Helbo overheard the conversation and added, "A man must respect and honor his wife, because all the blessings of a good home rest with her."

[TALMUDIC SOURCE: *Baba Metzia 59*]

Rabbi's Comment:

In this parable, the Talmud clearly explains how a man should treat his wife, and by implication, how a woman should treat her husband.

The rabbis believed that a happy home life is the basis for all goodness in the world. In a home with harmony and respect, parents and children will find joy and happiness. Where there is strife between a man and a woman, sorrow and sadness are certain to follow.

The Talmud emphasizes that the tone in the home ultimately depends on the level of mutual contentment. Hence, the prudent man treats his wife with the utmost honor and respect.

38. *Adam's* Rib

Rabban Gambiel, one of the greatest rabbinic authorities of his generation, was engaged in a heated debate with the emperor.

In a disparaging way, the emperor belittled Jewish beliefs by insulting his guest. "Your God is a thief," he declared.

The rabbi looked at him in disbelief.

"I can prove this to you by reading from the Book of Genesis," the emperor challenged.

"You have proof of that in the Bible?" the rabbi asked.

"Indeed I do. Look here, where it says, 'The Lord put Adam into a deep sleep, and while he slept, He removed one of his ribs and closed the flesh back into place.'

"That's my proof," the emperor announced. "The Lord took advantage of Adam by removing his rib without his knowledge. And all the while, Adam was unable to protect himself."

Meanwhile, the emperor's daughter, who had been listening to the argument, interrupted: "Father, that reminds me: You must notify the palace guard that a thief broke into the palace last night and stole a silver pitcher."

Before the emperor could reply, she added, "But don't worry, father. Although the thief took a silver pitcher, he left a gold pitcher in its place."

Astonished by the unexpected switch, the emperor exclaimed, "How wonderful to be blessed with such good fortune. There's no need for a palace guard. Such good luck should happen to us every night."

"Think about it, father," his daughter said. "Isn't this what happened to Adam? The Almighty One took a rib and in its place, gave him back a beautiful mate."

The emperor thought about what his daughter said, and

replied, "Well, God should not have taken the rib without Adam's knowledge."

"Oh, really?" his daughter said. Then turning to a servant, she ordered, "Go into the kitchen and bring me a piece of raw meat."

When the servant returned, she put the meat under her armpit, then offered it to her father. "Here, I want you to eat this."

"I will not!" the emperor sputtered in amazement. "How dare you insult me with such an offer!"

"Well," his daughter answered, "had God taken Adam's rib while he was awake, Eve, too, would have seemed appalling."

[TALMUDIC SOURCE: *Sanhedrin 39a*]

—◦◦◦—

Rabbi's Comment:

The daughter's response to the emperor's assertion is a perfect example of how the Talmud embraces enlightened views regarding women. In this parable, the emperor's daughter challenged the authority of her father and the impeccable logic of her argument swayed him. Intellectually, the daughter comes across as her father's equal. Another lesson derived from the story is that although upon first observation we might not understand the ways and the actions of the Divine, if we probe deeper into their meaning, we will find that God's ways are indeed correct.

—◦◦◦—

39. *Matchmaker, Matchmaker*

Rabbi Jose was once approached by a woman who asked, "Is it true that it took God only six days to create the world?"

"That is correct," he acknowledged.

"Tell me then, Rabbi," she inquired, "what has God been doing ever since that time?"

The woman's question caught the great rabbi by surprise. He pondered for a few brief moments, then replied with exuberance, "What else? Why God occupies Himself with matchmaking! Didn't you know that before each new birth, God must decide who will be married to whom? And this is no easy task. In fact, in God's eyes, it is as difficult as parting the Red Sea."

The woman did not believe that matchmaking was as difficult as Rabbi Jose had explained. And to prove him wrong, she decided to outdo the Creator. To do this, she paired off a thousand men with a thousand women, who, in turn, all married on a single day. She was delighted with her remarkable accomplishment, but her joy was short-lived. The following day, all two thousand men and women protested about being poorly matched.

The woman returned to Rabbi Jose and confessed, "You are right. Good marriages must indeed be made in Heaven."

"Yes," the rabbi agreed. "But no matter how well matched, a husband and wife must work hard to make their marriage work so that it may be consecrated here on earth."

[TALMUDIC SOURCE: *Pesikta Buber 11b–12a*]

Rabbi's Comment:

As successfully married couples know, a good marriage requires considerable effort. This applies not only to the selection of a mate, but to the subsequent effort both husband and wife must make as they strive to maintain their relationship. It is wise for every bride and groom to be aware of their partner's needs and desires and to be prepared to give them priority. Whatever may be the source of the magnetic attraction that brings two people together, the rabbis liked to believe there is a Divine hand behind it. This power of attraction has a spiritual dimension which shall be brought out and nurtured in the course of the marriage. The beauty of a good marriage is that the intimacy shared by two people creates a result greater than the sum of its parts.

40. Sour Grapes

Enticed by a crafty fox's exaggerated description of a Sabbath feast, a wolf invited himself to help the Jews in their preparation for the Sabbath. But upon entering the premises, the wolf was beaten by sticks and clubs.

The wolf managed to escape and was so angry with the fox that he decided to kill him. After a chase, the cornered fox begged: "Is it my fault that they beat you? They have a grudge against you because of your father.

"I happen to know that many years ago your father helped them prepare for their holiday celebrations, and then he ate all the choice goods placed on their table."

"Are you suggesting that I was beaten and punished as a result of a foolish mistake my father made?" exclaimed the wolf in anger.

The fox explained to the wolf that the children have not forgotten that by his father's hand their fathers had eaten sour grapes.

[TALMUDIC SOURCE: *Sanhedrin 38b*]

Rabbi's Comment:

Rabbi Meir, one of the great orators of his time, liked to tell this parable which teaches that a family reputation is passed from one generation to the next, and that heirs can be held accountable for the improprieties of their ancestors. Still, each new generation has an opportunity to learn from the mistakes of the past and start anew. We are destined to follow in the footsteps of our ancestors if we blind ourselves to their mistakes and shortcomings. By learning from the past, we avoid the possibility of having to repeat the mistakes we've made. Hence, Rabbi Meir reminds us that it is possible to turn the sourness of past generations into tomorrow's sweetness.

41. The True Heir

"You must be more careful with your amorous affairs," a mother warned her daughter. "After all, I don't want you to turn out like me."

"Like you, mother?" questioned the daughter.

"Yes," the woman confided. "I will share a secret with you. I have ten children, yet only one of them is the offspring of the man you call father." The woman's husband overheard this conversation, but said nothing. Years later, on his deathbed, he instructed that all his property go to his one child.

Following his death, confusion prevailed. His bereaved family was distraught. Each child wanted the right of inheritance, so they visited Rabbi Banaah to ask his advice.

"Go to your father's grave," he wisely told them. "Knock on it until he rises up. Then ask him to tell you what he meant."

Nine of his children went to the grave and banged on it, waiting to receive a sign. One child refused to show such disrespect and stayed at home.

Observing this, Rabbi Banaah announced, "This child is the true heir. The entire estate goes to him because he alone showed the proper respect for his father."

[TALMUDIC SOURCE: *Baba Batra 58a*]

Rabbi's Comment:

To Rabbi Banaah, it wasn't important which child had blood ties to the father. Instead, what mattered was the respect given to a parent, both in life and in memory. This respect demonstrates the highest love and devotion of a child. Here the Talmud teaches that the true heir to any man's property is the child or disciple who shows respect, regardless of ultimate personal gain. We also learn that the inheritance of values may matter more than what is inherited genetically.

42. The Deep Sleep

A man called Honi, the circle-drawer, was known far and wide for his miraculous ability to make rain. While traveling along a road, he saw a man planting a carob tree. "How long will it be before that tree bears fruit?" he inquired.

"Seventy years," replied the man.

"And what makes you think you will still be alive in seventy years to enjoy the fruit from that tree?"

"When I came into this world," the man answered, "I found full-grown carob trees that were planted by my forefathers. And like them, I am planting this tree for my children."

Shortly afterward, Honi ate a heavy meal and fell asleep. As he slept, a cave formed around Honi to hide him from by-passers. According to legend, the cave was so peaceful that Honi slept in it for seventy years. When he finally awoke, he saw an old man gathering carob fruit from a tree. He approached the man and said, "Didn't I see you plant this tree?"

"It would not be possible," the man said. "This tree was planted seventy years ago by my grandfather."

"Is it then possible," Honi said, "that I have been sleeping all that time?"

[TALMUDIC SOURCE: *Ta'anit 23a*]

Rabbi's Comment:

The Talmud urges each individual to consider that if his forefathers planted for him, and he found a lush world filled with plenty, he too must plan and plant for his children and his children's children, so that they can come into this world and discover the same plenty. This is the rabbinic reasoning against selfish, short-sighted people who say, "I will build, plant, and plan only for my own benefit." We found an abundant world when we entered it, and we have the responsibility of passing on the same world to future generations. This is one of the Talmud's finest ecological statements; note that it emphasizes humanity's responsibility for the environment. Each generation is dependent upon the previous one to take care of the planet and replenish what it has used up.

43. *True Inheritance*

Three sons were summoned to their father's deathbed. Quietly, the old man spoke his last words. To his first son, he said, "I leave a sack of dust to you."

Feebly nodding to his second son, he whispered, "And to you, I leave a sack of bones."

And to his third son: "I leave you a sack of feathers."

The three sons looked at each other in sad puzzlement. Not understanding their father's meaning, they asked Rabbi Banaah for an explanation. The wise rabbi pondered their tale for a few minutes.

He then asked, "Did your father own land?"

"Yes," one son answered.

"Did your father own cattle?"

"He did," another replied.

"And did he own many cushions and comforting garments?" the rabbi asked.

"Indeed," he was told.

"Well," Rabbi Banaah said, "it is quite clear that he was referring to these properties."

"But why leave us with this riddle?" one son asked.

"Your father wished for you to receive your inheritance on the conditions that you were clever enough to solve his riddle, or wise enough to ask someone for help."

The rabbi added: "It is obvious that your father desired to teach you an important lesson. While there are many problems with solutions, you may not be able to discern them on your own. And when you encounter such problems, there is no shame in seeking advice from others. Your father wanted you to know that, at times, the views of another may be more clear than your own. And lastly, he wished you to understand that no matter how wise you may be, there is always someone wiser."

[TALMUDIC SOURCE: *Baba Batra 58a*]

Rabbi's Comment:

A wise person not only knows the right answers, but also the right questions to ask. The rabbis liked to engage in give-and-take, and often found solutions to problems by deconstructing the issues and debating them. A rabbi willing to consult another, perhaps more knowledgeable person was considered very wise indeed.

44. *Partners in Creation*

"It is said that the creation of a child requires contributions from both husband and wife, as well as from God," a rabbi's disciple once said to him. "Specifically, what do each of these three partners contribute?"

"You have asked a very good question," the rabbi replied. "A child's bones, cartilage, nails, brain matter, and the whites of the eyes come from its father.

"The mother contributes such substances as skin, muscle, hair, pigment, and coloration of the body," he continued. "The color of the child's eyes, for example, is inherited from the mother."

"And then what comes from God?" one disciple questioned.

"The Holy One contributes the soul, a beautiful face, and the ability to see," the rabbi answered. "Also God provides such qualities as the capacity to hear, speak, walk, and think."

The learned rabbi added, "When a person's time comes to depart from this world, The Holy Blessed One redeems the things contributed by Heaven. Left behind are the contributions of the deceased's parents."

[TALMUDIC SOURCE: *Nidah 31a*]

Rabbi's Comment:

This parable teaches that after death, the physical characteristics our parents contribute belong to earth, but our soul and intellect are returned to God. This is a beautiful metaphor about the sacredness of every human life. Each of us is in part Divine and is therefore worthy of love, compassion, and respect.

HUMILITY

—◦◦◦—

45. The Appreciative Guest

To teach his students about appreciation, Rabbi Ben Zoma asked them to discern the difference between a good guest and a poor guest.

"What does a good guest express about his host?" the rabbi asked his students. "He says, 'Look at all the trouble my host has gone to on my behalf. How generous he is to place such a fine piece of meat on my dinner plate. He also fills my glass with wine, and he offers me many fine cakes. How fortunate I am to be his guest.'"

The rabbi then asked, "What does a poor guest express about his host? He says, 'What real effort is my host exerting on my behalf? All I am eating is a single slice of bread and one piece of meat, and with it, I am consuming only one glass of wine. Actually, my host had to go through the same effort so that his family would be fed, so I am simply an add-on, an afterthought to preparation which would have been necessary had I been his guest or not.'"

[TALMUDIC SOURCE: *Berachot 58a*]

Rabbi's Comment:

This parable is about arrogance and humility, and its interpretation is a matter of perspective. On the one hand, when the household preparations for a family meal are already in progress, a guest is indeed an add-on. This, however, does not negate the fact that it is a blessing to be invited and welcomed into another person's home. The invitation alone is an excellent reason to express appreciation. The hospitality most hosts extend to their guests is more abundant and generous than what they normally allot for themselves. Before a guest decides whether to take several servings or one, he should keep in mind that because he is served first, the host and his family must content themselves only with what remains. The arrogant person never feels enough has been done for him. Conversely, the humble person is appreciative of even the smallest gesture of good will.

46. *Honor Is Not an Option*

A heated debate among the rabbis caused a shift in leadership at the great academy in Babylonia. The debate was over the evening prayer: since there was no fixed time for it, was it optional or compulsory?

A student triggered the controversy by innocently asking Rabbi Joshua, "Is the evening prayer compulsory?"

"It is optional," replied Rabbi Joshua.

Then the student approached Rabban Gamaliel, head of the academy, with the same question. "It is compulsory," he answered.

"But Rabbi Joshua stated it was optional," the student replied in surprise.

"Let us wait until all the great sages assemble," Rabban Gamaliel told the student, "and we will settle this."

When all were assembled in the great academy's large hall, one rabbi stood and asked, "Is the evening prayer optional or compulsory?"

Sitting regally, Gamaliel spoke with authority: "It is absolutely compulsory." He paused before challenging, "Does anyone here dispute this?"

The rabbis were silent.

"What about you, Rabbi Joshua?" Gamaliel pressed. "I know you have contradicted me, advising it was optional. Stand before those who heard you and refute me now."

Joshua stood and replied, "If the witness were dead, I could refute the testimony, but since the witness and I are both alive, how can I deny what he says?"

Still seated, Rabban Gamaliel allowed Rabbi Joshua to stand while he lectured at length. Degrading assertions against Joshua upset the other sages, and soon varying arguments reverberated throughout the room. Many rabbis shouted at Gamaliel to stop his disgraceful display of shameful arrogance.

One rabbi rose and demanded, "How much longer must we endure Rabban Gamaliel's public insults of Rabbi Joshua?"

"We will not tolerate this," insisted another rabbi.

"Last New Year, Gamaliel insulted Joshua," someone added. "Then there was that debate over the firstborn with Rabbi Zadok. Then, too, Gamaliel was insolent. It is enough!"

One rabbi shouted, "Rabban Gamaliel must step down. He is unfit to head the academy."

"Who should replace him?" another asked. "Rabbi Joshua cannot because he is a party in the dispute."

Rabbi Akiba was mentioned, but someone claimed he had no ancestral merit and would fall under Gamaliel's curses.

"Let us appoint Rabbi Eliezer ben Azaria. He is fully qualified and is wise enough to address any question. He can afford to pay tribute to Caesar if necessary. And as he has descended from Ezra, he has ancestral merit."

When Rabbi Eliezer ben Azaria was asked to lead the academy, he said, "First, let me consult my family and specifically my wife."

His wife wondered, "What if someday they decide to oust you?"

"I believe it is still worthwhile," Eliezer said. "As the proverb states, 'Drink from the cup of honor this day, even though it may break tomorrow.' "

"Dear husband, you are not old enough," replied his wife. "You do not have even a single white hair."

Indeed, Eliezer ben Azaria was only eighteen years old, but that very day a miracle happened. Eighteen sections of his beard turned white!

"I suppose," he quipped, "that I am now about seventy years old! And my position has no time limitations."

As head of the academy, Eliezer banned every restriction set by Gamaliel regarding individuals who wished to study. Hundreds of new benches were brought in to accommodate the swell of new students.

[TALMUDIC SOURCE: *Berachot 27b*]

Rabbi's Comment:

Occasionally, power inspires arrogance. By distorting an honest dispute about a point of law, Rabban Gamaliel clearly overstepped his boundaries. As a result, the leadership and subsequent direction of the entire academy had changed. The sages and their disciples insisted that his public humiliation of others would no longer be tolerated. They insisted on having a spiritual leader who was above such pettiness.

Here, we learn that even a brilliant person such as Gamliel can be thwarted by arrogance, pride, and jealousy. Clearly, we should always reprimand in private and praise in public—never the reverse.

47. The Sting of Criticism

A bypasser overheard a conversation by three rabbis. Rabbi Judah said, "How wonderful are the works of the Romans. They have built markets, constructed bridges and magnificent bathhouses."

Rabbi Jose listened to his esteemed colleague's remarks, but remained silent.

"Please, please, you cannot convince me that the Romans do anything for the good of the people," Rabbi Simeon bar Yohai responded. "What they do is purely for their own benefit and self-aggrandizement. The Romans build marketplaces for their harlots. Their bathhouses are built so they can refresh themselves. And their bridges are used to collect tolls."

The eavesdropper listened intently and repeated what he heard to his family. They, in turn, repeated it to others, and their gossip soon spread to the Roman authorities.

The Romans reacted with a decree: "Judah, who complimented us, shall be honored by receiving the privilege to speak first on all occasions. Rabbi Jose, who had nothing to say, either good or bad, shall be exiled to the town of Sepphoris in upper Galilee. And Simeon bar Yohai, who was highly critical of us, shall be sentenced to death."

As soon as Simeon bar Yohai heard this verdict, he and his son sought refuge and fled to the academy, where they could hide and his wife could bring them food. When the Roman dragnet came too close, the father and son escaped, hiding in the caves of the hill country.

To their good fortune, a carob tree and a water well located at the mouth of the cave provided them with nourishment. All day long, the two men studied. To preserve their clothes, they sat naked in sand up to their necks. Only when they recited their prayers did they dress. They endured this austere life for twelve years.

Then they were approached by Elijah the prophet, who, standing at the cave's entrance, yelled to them, "I am here to inform you that Caesar has died, and your execution decree has been revoked."

Hearing this news, they joyfully came out of hiding. Shortly thereafter, they came across a man working in the fields. "Can you imagine that this man has given up the life of studying?" exclaimed Simeon bar Yohai. "Look at him. Instead, he prefers to toil so hard in the field." With those words, wherever Simeon bar Yohai or his son would cast their eyes, flames would occur. Then, a divine voice scolded them: "Did you emerge from your cave so you can criticize the world? Return to your cave at once!"

For an entire year, Simeon bar Yohai and his son repented. When they emerged from the cave, they vowed never to be critical again. They realized that devoting one's time entirely to study and prayer was not an option for everyone. They also understood the importance of how men and women must spend their time in labor so they could make a living. From then on, the two men only made kind remarks so that they might improve the world rather than pointing to faults in others.

[TALMUDIC SOURCE: *Shabbat 33b*]

Rabbi's Comment:

This parable reminds us that sharp words of criticism can be destructive because they are humiliating, demoralizing, hurtful, and insulting. Instead, it is the responsibility of those blessed with insight and understanding to provide constructive criticism through praise and encouragement. This parable also teaches that no one should search for faults in those who choose lifestyles different from his or her own.

48. *Kamsa and Bar Kamsa*

Legend says that the destruction of Jerusalem was due to a mix-up of two men having similar names. A certain well-respected man named Kamsa was invited by his good friend to attend a dinner party. The servant inadvertently delivered the invitation not to Kamsa but to another well-known resident of Jerusalem named Bar Kamsa, a man who happened to be the host's ardent enemy.

On the night of the party, the host saw Bar Kamsa enter.

"How dare you come here?" he declared, and ordered him to leave.

"Evidently I received your invitation by mistake," Bar Kamsa said. "But since I am here, let us both avoid embarrassment. Allow me to stay, and I will pay you for whatever I eat and drink."

"Absolutely not," the host refused.

"Allow me to stay," said the chagrined man, "and I will pay for half the party."

"No," the angry host insisted.

"Then I will pay the cost of the entire party," Bar Kamsa said. "Just don't allow either of us to be embarrassed."

The seething host, unable to tolerate the sight of Bar Kamsa, had him thrown out of the house.

Since the rabbis present at the event didn't intervene, Bar Kamsa assumed that they must have supported the host's behavior. Their passivity urged Bar Kamsa to plot retribution.

"I'll get even," Bar Kamsa vowed. "I will call down the wrath of the government."

Bar Kamsa went to Caesar, seeking revenge.

"Those Jews are rebelling against you," he lied.

"How can you prove this?" Caesar questioned.

"That will be easy," Bar Kamsa said. "Send them a calf to of-fer on their altar. They will insult you by refusing to accept your gift."

According to Jewish law, a blemished calf was unfit for sac-rifice. So while delivering the calf, Bar Kamsa wounded it. When the blemished calf was presented, the rabbis considered offering it—even with the blemish—to avoid insulting Caesar. They even discussed killing Bar Kamsa to prevent him from telling more lies to Caesar. They concluded, however, that no legal grounds for such excessive action existed and the calf was not used for the ritual sacrifice.

Could their rejection have been the catalyst that triggered Caesar's wrath against Israel that resulted in the destruction of Jerusalem and the Temple? We shall never know, but certainly the city was destroyed by Caesar.

With this, the Jewish community, led by Rabbi Yochanan, wept: "Due to the honesty of our rabbis, our temple is de-stroyed, our palace is burnt down, and we are exiled from our land; for lo, Jerusalem is destroyed."

[TALMUDIC SOURCE: *Gittin 55b*]

━━━◦◦◦◦━━━

Rabbi's Comment:

While historically this event was not the actual cause for Jerusalem's destruction by the Romans, the rabbis told the story to illustrate the importance of human tol-erance and the need to preserve the dignity of others, even that of enemies. Also, this parable warns that the consequences of humiliation and pain we inflict on others can be dire. Hence, the rabbis compared the public embarrassment of Bar Kamsa to an act that could result in cataclysmic retribution and destruction.

49. Wisdom Is Mightier Than the Sword

In his quest to rule the world, Alexander the Great led his mighty legion into the darkest part of Africa. To his surprise, he discovered a land solely inhabited by women.

As Alexander positioned his army to attack, the leader of the women shouted out to him: "If you kill us, people will say, 'He could do no better than to kill women.' "

Hmm, he thought. This woman is right.

"And if we kill you, your epitaph will read, 'He was killed by women.' "

"I will leave you in peace," he replied. "I request only that you bring me some bread."

Shortly thereafter, a loaf of bread made of pure gold was delivered to Alexander. It was placed before him on a gold pedestal.

After taking one look at the glittering prize and realizing that he could not eat it, he exclaimed, "What kind of people are you who eat gold bread?"

"You have come a great distance to get bread from us," a woman answered. "Have you no bread in your own land?"

Legend tells us that when Alexander departed, he inscribed on the gate of the land of women, "I, Alexander of Macedonia, was a fool until I traveled to Africa and visited this province. Here is where I learned true counsel from women."

[TALMUDIC SOURCE: *Tamid 32a*]

Rabbi's Comment:

If the women of the land had responded to Alexander's request by actually bringing an edible loaf of bread, they would be acknowledging their subservience to him. They did not wish to antagonize Alexander by refusing his request, so they responded by providing a gift that was symbolic of their autonomy and courage. The women gained advantage by reinterpreting a symbol of military conquest and transforming it to fit their agenda. Thus, the women demonstrated that while they may not have been as powerful as their enemy in military assets, they were superior in their political acumen.

The rabbis liked to teach by using men who were larger than life as examples. Alexander the Great was one. This parable illustrated that the power of reasoning can stop even the mightiest army. Alexander is essentially conquered by the logic and wisdom of the women he encountered, but he was wise enough to acknowledge this fact. The Talmud reminds us that no one should fear learning from others. The truly wise person knows that gender makes no difference in the application of truth and insight.

COMPASSION

---◦◦◦---

50. The Price of Hesitation

A beloved teacher, Nahum, was totally blind, his legs and arms were cut off, and his body was covered with boils and sores. The former great scholar lived in a dilapidated shack, and the legs of his bed stood in bowls of water to protect him from ants.

To alleviate some of his misery, Nahum's students planned to remove him from the house full of refuse. They would move their teacher where he would be safer.

"My children," Nahum said to them, "first remove my meager possessions; then you may carry me from the house. I assure you, as long as I am inside, the house will not collapse."

They obeyed his instructions, and no sooner than he was carried outside, the shack did indeed fall.

"Teacher," one student said, "you are a wholly righteous, pious man. Why has this misery befallen you?"

I brought this upon myself," he replied. "Years ago, when I traveled to visit my father-in-law, I met a poor man begging for food. I led three mules, one laden with food, another with drink, and a third groaning under piles of delicacies. So I told the beggar, 'Wait until I unpack, and I will feed you.'

"But I acted too slowly, because while I unloaded the food, the man died from hunger. I was so contrite, I fell upon the man, covering him with my body, and proclaimed, 'May my eyes that were blind to your immediate needs become blind. May my hands which had no pity on your hands be severed, and may my legs which had no pity on your legs be cut off.'

"Even so, I thought my punishment too light, so I added, 'May my body be covered with boils.' "

Nahum's disciples could not comprehend why their master should suffer so deeply. One cried out, "Woe to us, that we should find you in such a sad and awful state."

"No, my students," Nahum replied. "Woe to me if you did not find me thus. For although I suffer, I am content, knowing I repented for missing the opportunity to save a life."

[TALMUDIC SOURCE: *Ta'anit 21a*]

Rabbi's Comment:

This parable has two lessons. First, when there is an opportunity to relieve the suffering of another, we must respond quickly. Although Nahum acted nobly, he reacted slowly. Consequently, a man who could have been saved died. As Nahum points out, even though he was genuinely willing to help, the desire alone was insufficient. Nahum believed his lack of empathy cost the man his life; he simply waited too long to assess the severity of suffering before offering to help.

The second lesson is that sincere contrition is more

than just an act of repentance. Nahum's shame in failing to respond promptly created a powerful example of true humility and penitence. To Nahum, a human life was so precious that he was willing to forfeit his own well-being to obtain forgiveness. It reminded his students that a wholly righteous and pious person finds his own well-being secondary to that of others.

51. A Person of Character

The rabbis were discussing which qualities are to be considered in evaluating a person's character. After a heated debate, Rabbi Ilyah volunteered to conclude the discussion.

"So we can agree," he said, "that b'koso (by his cup), b'keeso (by his pocket), and b'kaahso (by his anger), a person's character can be determined."

The other rabbis looked at each other and laughed. "It is true that b'koso, b'keeso and b'kaahso sound alike," one of them said. "But this serious discussion deserves to be resolved by more than a silly rhyme."

"Aha!" Rabbi Ilyah exclaimed. "Let me explain. The cup is significant, because we can tell how hospitable a man is by the way he fills the cup of others. And certainly, how much he drinks is a clear indication of his values. So too by whether or not a man sees his own cup of life as half full or half empty.

"We can learn from his pockets his willingness to take from his means to help others.

"Then too," the wise rabbi continued, "the way he controls his anger tells us about his gentleness and tolerance for others."

His colleagues laughed and nodded. One man added, "And may our laughter remind you that it is said that a person can be judged by his laughter, too."

"Is that so?" asked Rabbi Ilyah.

"Yes," the man replied. "A person can be judged by how readily he laughs with others and at himself."

[TALMUDIC SOURCE: *Eruvin 65b*]

Rabbi's Comment:

Hospitality, generosity, and an even temper are fine qualities, and one who possesses all of them is an exceptional person. An individual of such character usually finds it easy, if not always comfortable, to laugh at himself. Also, he never laughs at others, but always laughs along with them.

52. Food for Thought

A man of great wealth and scholarship owned a large warehouse of food. During a time of scarcity, he decided to share his abundance with others.

He made an announcement to the people. "The food I store is free to those of you who are students of the Torah, those who have studied the Mishna, the Gemara, the law or the narratives. But the ignorant do not have permission to enter my warehouse."

Infuriated, one man pushed his way to the front of the large crowd and demanded, "Master, give me some food!"

"Have you studied the Torah?" he was asked.

"No."

"Well, are you a student of the Mishna or any of the other topics I mentioned?"

"I am not," the man answered staunchly.

"Well, then, why should I feed you?"

"Feed me as the dog or the raven would be fed," he exclaimed. "For as God provides food for these creatures, so should you!"

The warehouse owner gave food to the young man and sent him off.

That night, he said to his son, "I actually gave food to that ignoramus. How could I have done such a thing?"

"Did you not recognize that young man?" his son asked. "He was disguised in rags, but he is actually a student of yours. That man was Rabbi Jonathan Ben Amram."

"Why would he put on such a charade?"

"He studies for the pure honor of studying," the son answered. "Jonathan would not want to gain anything of material value from his study of the texts."

Once the warehouse owner was aware of Jonathan's motives, his attitude changed. From then on, he vowed to help anyone who was in need, and indeed, he assumed the responsibility of providing food to any person who was hungry.

In making his decision, the warehouse owner followed what he had learned from his studies: "If a person lives in a place for thirty days, he is responsible for contributing to the soup kitchen. If he lives in the same place for three months, he is responsible for contributing to the charity box to help the less fortunate. If he lives in the same place for six months, he must contribute to the clothing fund, and for nine months, to the burial fund for indigents. And if a person lives in the same place for one year, he must contribute to the repair and maintenance of the town wall."

[Talmudic source: *Baba Batra 8a*]

Rabbi's Comment:

Each individual is responsible for another. There can be no artificial distinctions between any of us when it comes to times of need.

Each human being should be recognized as someone sacred. Those people who are fortunate enough to have an abundance of wealth have the responsibility of sharing their good fortune with those who are in need. Acts of generosity emulate the Divine Image.

53. The Measure of a Mensch

While discussing the characteristics of a *mensch*, Rabbah asked Rafram bar Papa, "What do you recall about Rabbi Huna?"

"I know nothing about his childhood," bar Papa said, "but I know of the wonderful acts in his life. Truly, he was a mensch.

"For example, on overcast and stormy days, he often traveled about in his golden coach. Huna inspected the village walls, and if any were beyond repair, he ordered them knocked down. If an owner could afford a new wall, he was responsible for the expense. But if he could not, Rabbi Huna would pay for the wall himself.

"And did you know that on Friday afternoons," bar Papa continued, "just before the Sabbath, Huna sent a messenger to the market to purchase any unsold vegetables. After buying the vegetables, Huna had them dumped into the river."

"Why did he have the vegetables thrown into the river?" asked Rabbah.

"During the week, if a farmer brought too much food, he could sell it the next day," bar Papa said. "But on Fridays, because of the Sabbath, it couldn't be sold until Sunday, which meant the vegetables would wilt or spoil. By protecting the farmers against loss, they were more willing to bring more goods to the market on Fridays."

"Why didn't Huna distribute the vegetables to the poor?" Rabbah asked.

"If he did that," bar Papa replied, "the poor would come to depend upon his generosity and lose their incentive to care for themselves."

"Why, then, didn't he give the vegetables to the animals?" Rabbah inquired.

"Rabbi Huna believed vegetables were intended for human

consumption," bar Papa explained, "and feeding them to animals might insult the poor, or even show disrespect to God's bountiful gifts to humanity."

Continuing his story, bar Papa said, "There were times when Huna would purchase a new medicine and keep it in a water bag in front of his house. He invited all those in need to take what they wanted.

"And before sitting down to a meal, Rabbi Huna would first call out from his doorway, 'Whoever is hungry, come and join me.' He kept a jug of water at his door for guests to wash their hands before meals, preventing the spread of disease through uncleanliness."

"What a wonderful man he was," Rabbah exclaimed.

"Yes," claimed bar Papa, "he went far beyond anything I could possibly do."

[TALMUDIC SOURCE: *Ta'anit 20b*]

Rabbi's Comment:

Generosity and charitable deeds have always been the hallmark of a learned individual. While acquiring knowledge is always praiseworthy, individuals held in highest esteem are those who treat others with kindness and respect. Although intellectual growth was considered the greatest of all pursuits, it is never an end in itself. The person who was able to transform learning into good deeds was regarded as a true mensch.

54. The Ambiguity of Tradition

Sometimes a simple misunderstanding about another culture can cause grave consequences. Such was the case of Baitar, a small village in southern Israel, that was destroyed by the Romans. How could such a terrible thing come about?

One day a Roman emperor's daughter was being escorted through Baitar when her travel chair broke. The bearers found one of its posts cracked, and they cut down a nearby cedar tree to replace it. Woefully, the Roman travelers were unaware that they had committed a trespass.

In Israel, it was a custom to plant a cedar tree when a boy is born; for a girl, a pine tree. When a child married, the tree was cut down and its branches used to make a chupah. The residents of Israel believed the fate of every young adult was reflected by the growth of his or her tree.

The villagers were infuriated by the destruction of the cedar. Heated words were exchanged, and an argument quickly escalated into a fight. The Romans were beaten and the emperor's daughter was unable to escape injury. When the emperor heard about the incident, he pronounced it a full-scale rebellion. In retaliation, he dispatched troops to destroy the entire village.

When the massacre ceased, so many men, women, and children were slaughtered that the streams in the village ran with blood. For years thereafter, the waters were so red they could be used only for farming; not only for irrigation, but as a fertilizer, as well.

[TALMUDIC SOURCE: *Gittin 57a*]

Rabbi's Comment:

Sadly, the beautiful custom of planting a tree to celebrate a child's birth yielded a terrible calamity. This tragedy of misunderstanding could have been averted. Had the conquering Romans been more sensitive to local culture and customs, their ignorance would not have triggered such awful excess. Likewise, the people of Baitar could have averted a catastrophe had they tempered their anger. The villagers should not have put the burden of knowledge on the Romans. They should have viewed the cutting of the tree not as an act of malice but as an inadvertent misunderstanding. In this instance, the indifference resulted in bloodshed, but more commonly, the indifference toward a neighbor's religious and cultural expression is considered simply offensive.

55. The Rowdy Neighbors

Nothing was more pleasurable to Rabbi Meir than the time he spent studying the Torah and teaching it to his students in the quiet, peaceful confines of his home.

His bliss ended, however, when a group of rowdy hooligans moved next door. Night and day, they disturbed him. They were so distracting that no matter how much Rabbi Meir tried to ignore them, he was unable to concentrate on his studies. Their noise was ruining his life.

In despair, he resorted to prayer—a tactic he at first had hesitated to use, even though he was convinced it would work.

Having determined that there was no way to be rid of the neighbors, he prayed for their death.

His wife Beruriah overheard his prayers and exclaimed, "My dear husband, how could you do such a thing? You are actually praying for these people to die! What gives you the right to request such an awful event? And what makes you even think your prayers will be answered?"

The rabbi answered, "Doesn't it say in the Book of Psalms that all sinners should be eliminated from the world? If only these neighbors would die, their rowdiness would cease, and I could study in peace and quiet once again."

"No, you have completely misunderstood the words of the Book of Psalms," his wise wife said. "It doesn't say that all the sinners should be eliminated. It says that their sins should be eliminated."

She took out the Book of Psalms and read a passage from it to her husband. "You see, my loving husband, when their sins end, there will be no more wicked people in the world. So do not pray for these sinners to die. Instead, have mercy on them. Pray for them to realize their shortcomings and change their ways. Then, you and all of our neighbors will have peace, and the sinners will have inner peace as well."

Rabbi Meir concurred that his wife was right. So he began to pray on his rowdy neighbors' behalf, that they might improve themselves and find inner peace.

He prayed for them, and they heard his prayers. They were so moved that they began to respect his need for quiet, and soon serenity was restored to the neighborhood. Just as it is written in the Book of Psalms, "the wicked were no more."

[TALMUDIC SOURCE: *Berachot 10a*]

Rabbi's Comment:

We should never attempt to solve a negative problem with a negative response. To attack anger with anger is a poor solution.

We must be merciful toward others rather than attempt to obliterate them. It is better to eliminate offensive behavior by teaching good behavior. We must not feel superior to others or, if we are stronger, use force to overcome them. Instead, through acts of goodness and mercy, we should respect their capacity to change for the well-being of others.

56. Sharp Words

When Resh Lakish saw Rabbi Yochanan bathing in the Jordan River, he jumped in to join him.

"You should be as energetic in your study of the Torah as you are in the way you play in the river," Yochanan said.

Eyeing Yochanan slyly, Resh Lakish retorted, "And your beauty should only be reserved for a woman."

"In that case," Yochanan said, "if I can convince you to engage in a life of study, I will give you my sister in marriage; she is even prettier than I."

Now Resh Lakish had never been a scholar and, in fact, had a poor reputation in the village. To many, he was considered untrustworthy. But Yochanan inspired him to study the Torah. In time, like his mentor, Resh Lakish became a worthy scholar.

Years later, the two men met at the study house and became engaged in a heated debate. Although no one remembers why they were arguing, Rabbi Yochanan quipped, "Well, I suppose a thief knows his trade."

Resh Lakish replied, "Although I have changed my ways and have become a student of the Torah, I am still regarded as the person I formerly was. If this is so, I must assume that I have benefited nothing from your teachings."

"I remind you," Yochanan answered, "that I taught you the laws of God."

The conversation ended abruptly. Obviously hurt, Yochanan was unable to continue and left the study house.

Resh Lakish realized then how deeply he had hurt his teacher. Ridden with guilt, he became gravely ill. Despondent beyond recovery, he died of a broken heart.

Hearing of his student's death, Rabbi Yochanan was stricken with grief. It is said that he never recovered from his estrangement from Resh Lakish and went to his grave with the same guilt.

[TALMUDIC SOURCE: *Baba Batra 84a*]

—◦◦◦—

Rabbi's Comment:

This parable reminds me of the words of an unknown poet, recited to me by my mother: "Words like arrows fly. Go and catch them if you try."

Rabbi Yochanan and Resh Lakish were brilliant scholars, and each had a sharp, quick tongue. They possessed considerable legal reasoning, their decisions were inspired, and they had the power to wound with their words. Here, the Talmud teaches how devastating malicious words can be. We witness how two otherwise well-meaning, brilliant scholars inflicted irreversible harm with their cunning, caustic remarks. Although neither meant to inflict serious harm on the other, once spoken, harsh words made a deep wound.

On the other hand, while insults are by nature offensive, they are not always unforgivable. Rabbi Yochanan could have been more sensitive to Resh Lakish's remorse, especially as he became ill with despair. Sadly, Yochanan also suffered remorse, but only when it was too late. Consequently, he was riddled with guilt for the rest of his life.

This parable teaches us that words are, indeed, like arrows, capable of piercing another's heart. The Talmud reminds us to choose our words carefully as we express our opinions, and to be mindful of the feelings of others, particularly those individuals who have worked hard to improve themselves. Do not hold a person's past against him or her, the parable warns, as the individual facing you today may be completely different from what he or she was yesterday.

57. The Visit

When the revered rabbinic sage Rabbi Kahanna heard that Rabbi Helbo was seriously ill, he was disheartened to learn that no one had visited his sick friend. This prompted Kahanna to return to the house of study where he could teach his students about the importance of visiting the infirmed and spending time with them.

"Do you not recall when one of Rabbi Akiba's students became gravely ill, and the scholars and sages failed to visit him?" Kahanna declared. "The great Rabbi Akiba himself visited the ailing student. He instructed the people to sweep the ground around the sick man's bed and to sprinkle it with water.

"The student was revived by these kind ministrations, and following his illness, he said to Rabbi Akiba: 'My great teacher, by your visit, you have given me life.'

"Rabbi Akiba promptly returned to the study house, and from that day admonished his students to visit the ill and infirm.

"He taught, 'Whoever does not visit the sick is like one who sheds their blood.' "

[TALMUDIC SOURCE: *Nedarin 39b*]

Rabbi's Comment:

One of the most important commandments in the Torah is "The Mitzvah of Bikur Cholim," which teaches the importance of visiting the ill and infirm. Each of us should welcome the opportunity to bring cheer and comfort to revive the heart and spirit of the ailing.

We don't have to be physicians to minister to a patient. The combination of medicine, therapy, prayer, and the care of loved ones augments the healing process. Anyone familiar with a sickbed surely appreciates the benefit of their friends' and family's visits.

58. The Hillel-Shammai Debate

Rabbi Abba tells a story about an ongoing, three-year argument between the school of Hillel and the school of Shammai regarding the application of the Talmudic law. At the heart of the debate was which school's interpretation was more valid.

In the midst of the debate, a voice from Heaven announced that both schools conveyed the words of the living God. Following a sigh from both sides, the voice added that the law is in agreement with the decisions of the school of Hillel.

Naturally, there was rejoicing from the Hillel scholars, coupled with disappointment from the Shammai representatives. The ambiguous response of the voice from Heaven led all parties to consider another question: "If both schools conveyed God's word, why was Hillel chosen as a greater authority over Shammai?"

The sages quickly responded: "The Hillel scholars were kind and humble. They also displayed respect by their willingness to study the rulings of both schools and exhibited considerable modesty when they described the decisions of Shammai before their own."

"There is a simple but important lesson in this," said Rabbi Abba. "The Holy, Blessed One elevates all who humble themselves. Likewise, God humbles all who elevate themselves."

"All who chase after greatness find greatness fleeing from them," the sages added. "But those who hide from greatness are found by greatness. Time is forced back for all who are anxious and impatient. Yet those who allow time to work on their behalf find time standing in wait for them."

{TALMUDIC SOURCE: *Eruvin 13b*}

Rabbi's Comment:

Historically, the schools of Hillel and Shammai remained rivals throughout Talmudic discourse. The decisions of Hillel were generally more lenient, forgiving, and gentle in comparison to the stricter rulings of Shammai.

In this parable, Rabbi Abba in the name of his teacher, Rabbi Samuel, reminds us that it is preferable to be more liberal and accepting of human limitations with respect to the application of the law. We should remember to embrace not only the letter but the intent of the law, which broadens to accommodate the frailties and weaknesses of real life. It is only when we stray from its intent that the law does not serve us well.

59. The Dream of Wine

"I had a dream last night," one rabbi told another. "It confuses me because I do not understand it."

"Tell me about your dream," his friend asked.

"In my dream, my friends and I were all drinking beer, and later we started drinking hard liquor. Then we were enjoying a delicious wine, and finally I woke up. Tell me, what do you think my dream means?" the rabbi inquired.

"It's a good sign to dream about alcoholic drinks," the second rabbi answered. "But with wine, there's a special significance."

"What's so special about wine?"

"With wine, you never know what may happen. Sometimes, something positive will occur, and other times, you'll experience something negative.

"You see, wine is like life itself," the rabbi continued. "As we learn in the Psalms, 'Wine gladdens the heart of man.' And in Proverbs, we learn, 'Give wine to one whose soul is bitter.' So you see, you just never know what may result."

"What you say is correct," the first rabbi said, "but it doesn't apply to those of us who are scholars. For in our case, wine is always a good sign, because we welcome others to eat our bread and drink our wine. We are always eager to share our wine so others may share our enjoyment."

At first, the second rabbi remained silent. After contemplating what his friend had said, he concurred, "You are right. Wine is always a good sign. So let the world strive to be scholars like us, because our hearts are gladdened by sharing and our spirits are never bitter."

[TALMUDIC SOURCE: *Berachot 57*]

Rabbi's Comment:

Psalm 104, which reads, "Wine gladdens the heart of man," is often quoted by the rabbis to teach several important lessons. First, it teaches that wine is never to be used as an intoxicant, removing us from the reality of life. Instead, its purpose is to complement life, enhancing the ordinary pleasures of living. As an intoxicant used to get drunk, however, it can embitter the soul; but used properly, wine provides joy and gladness.

The image of wine serves as a metaphor for rabbinic learning and scholarship. It is true that knowledge may not bring perfect results in every single situation. But in the case of true scholars, knowledge offered with affection and respect is certain to enhance the lives of others. For this reason, the second rabbi ultimately comes to view a dream about wine as a good sign. Like wine, good scholarship rejuvenates the heart of humanity.

HARMONY

―⟳―

60. The People's Choice

In a conversation concerning the appointment of a community leader, Rabbi Isaac stressed that the appointment should be made only after consulting the people. He told his colleagues that once a worthy individual is identified, the people are more likely to follow and be inspired by him if they are asked to be involved in his appointment.

"Let me cite an example," Rabbi Isaac said. "When God chose Bezalel to design and build the tabernacle in the wilderness, The Almighty first consulted with Moses.

" 'Do you consider Bezalel a proper choice?' God asked Moses.

" 'God, I am honored that you ask my opinion,' said Moses. 'But certainly if you think he is suitable, then I must agree.'

" 'Even so,' God said, 'go ask the people.'

"So Moses consulted the people of Israel and asked them to consider Bezalel. 'If God thinks Bezalel should build the tabernacle, and you, Moses, agree, then we must agree as well,' the people responded. 'Bezalel is our choice.' "

Rabbi Samuel Ben Nachmanai said, "When the consent of the people was sought, Bezalel was chosen because of his reputation as a man of great wisdom.

"God grants wisdom to those who are already wise," he added.

[TALMUDIC SOURCE: *Berachot 55*]

———✧✧✧———

Rabbi's Comment:

In an ancient time when rulers claimed to have divine right, the concept of seeking communal consent was unprecedented. The Israelites, however, recognized that it was desirable for their leaders to have the approval of the ruling class—which included even those leaders who were believed to have been designated by God.

This parable is an account of a fictitious discussion between God and Moses, and it reflects the contemporary, scholarly debate on the methods used to designate authority. It also teaches an important lesson about the value of inviting people to participate in the decision-making process prior to the implementation of a new undertaking. People who are involved during the early stages of any new project are more likely to give their consent and support as the planning for the project is honed over time.

———✧✧✧———

61. People Need People

As multitudes of people walked up the broad stairway leading to the temple in Jerusalem, Rabbi Ben Zoma offered the following blessing: "Blessed is the intellect that solves all mystery, and blessed is the Creator who provided all these people to serve me."

When his students heard the rabbi's blessings, they did not understand how he could say something so arrogant. After all, their teacher was known for his humility. Finally, one man mustered the nerve to ask the rabbi to explain his words.

"Imagine the enormous difficulty the first human being had trying to eat even a simple piece of bread," Ben Zoma told his students. "Just think of all the tasks he was required to execute. First he had to plow, and then he had to sow. Afterwards, he reaped. Next he had to bind the sheaves. Then, he had to thresh, winnow, and separate the grain.

"Still, there was more. He then had to grind the grain into flour, sifting it so it would be fine. After that, he kneaded the flour. Finally the bread was baked, and at last he was able to eat and enjoy the loaf that he had made."

After a slight pause, the rabbi added, "But as for me, I have only to get up each morning from a good night's sleep, and I eat bread. I didn't have to labor like the first man did, because everything has already been done for me.

"Likewise, think what the first human being had to do so that he could wear a simple garment to cover himself," the rabbi continued. "He had to shear the wool, wash it, comb it, and then spin it into yarn. Once he had the yarn, he had to weave it and fashion it into a garment to wear. Again, all I must do is get up each morning and choose which garment to wear. All that the first man had to do by himself has been done for me by many others.

"Now think about the different skilled craftspeople who come to the front door of my house," the rabbi told his students. "Because of them, I don't even need to travel to the marketplace. Look at all the things I have in my house that require difficult, time-consuming effort and diverse skills, yet others do these things for me.

"How fortunate I am that the Intellect of the universe, which understands all mysteries, has provided these skilled, knowledgeable people to serve my needs."

The rabbi lowered his head and said softly, "I do not wish to be arrogant. Instead I wish to remain mindful of the blessings that make my life so much easier. And with the time I save due to the labor of others, I am grateful to pursue what I love most, the study of the Talmud."

[TALMUDIC SOURCE: *Berachot, page 58a*]

―≈≈≈―

Rabbi's Comment:

When first spoken, the students interpreted Rabbi Ben Zoma's blessing as arrogance, but instead, he delivered a message of appreciation for all humankind.

Although Rabbi Ben Zoma's lesson on appreciation was taught many hundreds of years ago, it still resonates today. In the modern world, each of us is the recipient of goods and services provided by a vast number of people. Consider, for example, the thousands of workers who contribute their intellect as well as their toil to the building of an automobile. Look around any house or office and mentally list the countless people who were required to produce the thousands of items under its roof. It would be impossible for one human being to own so many objects, many of which come from around the world, were it not for the proficiency and labor of others. When you consider the human energy and time required to create and produce the things we enjoy, we have much for which to be thankful. As the world's population continues to grow, so does our need to rely on others.

62. Healing Hands

Rabbi Yochanan sat by the bedside of his sick friend, Rabbi Hiyyah. "I see how you suffer," he said to his ailing companion. "Give me your hand."

The two men held hands, and instantaneously Rabbi Hiyyah was healed.

Not long thereafter, Rabbi Yochanan himself became ill. His friend Rabbi Hanina paid him a visit. And when Rabbi Hanina held his hand, Rabbi Yochanan was immediately healed.

The story about the healing of the rabbis spread from village to village. When people heard what transpired, the question was asked, "If Rabbi Yochanan had the power in his hands to heal, why was he unable to heal himself?"

The rabbis answered, "Just as one who is in prison cannot free himself from his confinement, a patient usually requires a doctor to cure himself of illness."

[TALMUDIC SOURCE: *Berachot 5b*]

Rabbi's Comment:

This parable points to the close bonds the rabbis shared with each other. It also emphasizes that we have the capacity to solve other people's problems even though we may not see clearly through our own. It's important to remember that even the most astute person is sometimes unable to solve his or her own dilemmas.

For this reason, we must have the courage to seek help from others. This is a simple reminder that people need people.

63. Four Types of Students

A group of learned rabbis were discussing their students, whom they were teaching about the law.

One rabbi said, "In my opinion, the most difficult type of student is like a funnel. This student retains nothing. Whatever goes in one ear comes out the other."

The second rabbi said, "I think the most disappointing type of student is one who resembles a strainer. The most important information that passes through his mind escapes, and he retains from his lesson only what is superfluous or insignificant. Therefore, he is even worse off than if he had retained nothing. This student is like wine that is strained: the sediment is retained while the wine, which should be consumed, passes through, and is wasted."

The third rabbi said, "My favorite type of student is like a sponge. This individual is capable of absorbing everything he is taught."

The fourth rabbi said, "I think the most satisfying student to teach is like a sieve. He allows insignificant information to pass through, retaining only quality material. This student is like a sieve in which grains of wheat are shaken to eliminate dust and chaff, retaining only the finer inner kernel."

[TALMUDIC SOURCE: *Prike Avot 5*]

Rabbi's Comment:

Anyone who's ever attempted to teach knows that students fall into one of these four categories. Students who resemble the funnel and strainer exasperate and disappoint their teachers. But it is a joy to teach students who are like sponges and sieves. They renew a teacher's faith in the human intellect and in the next generation's capacity to absorb information, which, in turn, can be passed along to future generations. Observing such passing of knowledge is a teacher's richest reward.

64. The Miraculous Human Body

One day the rabbis were discussing the marvels of the human body, and how each organ contributes to a person's well-being and character.

They agreed that the kidneys provide counsel, the heart discerns, the tongue shapes the words, and the mouth pronounces them.

The gullet takes in, and sometimes spits out, all manner of food; the windpipe produces the voice. The lungs absorb moisture, and the liver is the center of anger.

The gallbladder softens anger; the spleen produces laughter. The large intestine grinds the food. The stomach induces sleep, and the nose awakens.

The rabbis agreed that should the nose fail to wake us and remain asleep, or the stomach chooses to stay awake, a person would waste away. And if both organs brought on sleep, or simultaneously kept a person awake, surely death would result.

[TALMUDIC SOURCE: *Berachot 61a*]

Rabbi's Comment:

Wisely, the rabbis taught that every feature of the human body was created with a special purpose. Meticulously designed, each part has a specific function that benefits the entire organism. Should one organ stray from its intended function, the entire body is jeopardized.

The rabbis believed the human body is miraculous, and understood that it functions as a fully integrated system much like a human community. In this respect, the human body serves as a metaphor for human behavior and social order; for a harmonious society, members must work together, each individual contributing to the well-being of the whole. By this rationale, a single member who disrupts the entire group jeopardizes everyone's well-being.

Given today's new interest in holistic medical treatments, the wisdom of the ancient rabbis seems especially perennial.

65. Twice Cured

Once the great rabbinic sage Rabbah became very ill.

Rabbah summoned his servants and said, "I beg of you, tell no one of my infirmity. I worry that people will gossip about me should my illness be known. This could adversely affect my usual good fortune."

The rabbi added, "Should my illness, however, linger for several more days, tell everyone in the marketplace. This will accomplish two things. First, my enemies will be pleased. Since we have been taught not to rejoice when our enemies fall, God will be unhappy with them. To spite my enemies, he will heal me.

"Secondly, those who have concern for my well-being will pray for me. And through their prayers, God will send great blessings.

"Thus, I will be doubly cured."

[TALMUDIC SOURCE: *Nedarin 40a*]

Rabbi's Comment:

In a course of a lifetime, we all acquire supporters and detractors—those who love us and care about our well-being, and those who do not. This parable teaches us to recognize the purpose and value of all relationships we encounter in life, even the negative ones. We can benefit from everyone we know, even our enemies.

66. The Captives

While visiting Mount Carmel, two pious Jews were taken prisoner. They walked toward a faraway land, their captor behind them.

"Do you see that camel ahead?" one Jew said to his companion. "It is blind in one eye. And those two barrels on its back? One is filled with wine and the other with oil."

"You are right," his friend replied. "And look at the two men leading the camel. One is a Jew and the other is not."

Their captor overheard the conversation and was unable to maintain his silence.

"You impudent people," he shouted at them. "We are fifty paces behind those two men and that camel. How could you claim to know such things?"

"Not only are we correct," one Jew said, "we can prove it."

"If you can, I will set you free."

The two prisoners looked at each other and smiled. One began, "See how the camel only eats herbs on one side of the road. That's because he can only see out of one eye. He cannot see the other side of the road.

"Now observe those two barrels. Both are dripping liquid. The wine that leaks from the one barrel is quickly absorbed by the earth. The oil that leaks from the other puddles on the ground. Look at your feet, and you'll see."

Undaunted, the captor demanded, "How can you possibly know one of these two men is a Jew?"

The prisoner explained, "Notice how the non-Jew attends to his needs in the roadway, while the Jew steps to the side for some privacy."

The captor scurried ahead to examine the camel and the two men, and found that his prisoners' observations were correct.

Sighing in defeat, he liberated them, kissed their heads, and welcomed them to a banquet in their honor at his house.

As he danced in delight before them, he offered this toast: "Blessed is the One who chose the seed of Abraham to receive discernment; for no matter where they go, they seize the moment and overtake even the mightiest captors with their princely ways of wisdom."

[TALMUDIC SOURCE: *Sanhedrin 104b*]

Rabbi's Comment:

In this parable, two intelligent men outwitted their enemy by simply observing and interpreting bare facts. They only had to pay attention to obvious physical evidence and rely on what they had learned in the past to assess the situation.

Once again we learn that it is not the strength of the hand but the power of observation and intellect that wins the day. The astonishing mind may perceive very clearly what brute force will take for granted.

67. Extreme Patience

In a heated argument, two men debated whether it was possible for anyone to make the great rabbinic sage Hillel lose his temper.

"I can," said one of the men.

"I'll bet you four hundred zuzim that you cannot."

"It's a bet. You just wait here and watch what I do," the one man told his friend.

Since it was late in the afternoon on Friday, the eve of the Sabbath, the man went directly to Rabbi Hillel's house. Well aware that it was a custom for most people to bathe in preparation for the holy day of rest, the man knocked on Hillel's door at the precise moment when he knew Hillel would be bathing.

His head still soaked in shampoo, Hillel came to the door. "What is it you want?" he said.

"I have an important question to ask."

"So ask," the rabbi said.

"Tell me, Rabbi, why are the heads of the Babylonians shaped so round, like a ball?"

"My dear man," Hillel responded, "you have asked an interesting question. The answer has to do with the poor care that a Babylonian infant receives at birth. That is what causes them to have round heads."

With that, the man thanked him and walked away. A few minutes later he came back and again knocked on Hillel's door.

When Hillel greeted him, the man stated that he had yet another question to ask.

"Ask, my friend."

"I must know why the Palmyreans have squinty eyes that always appear crossed."

"My son, it is because they live in the sand dunes and the

sun is constantly reflecting off the grains of sand into their eyes," Hillel patiently replied.

The man left again, but shortly thereafter knocked once more on Hillel's door.

"Rabbi Hillel," the man demanded, "I have a terribly pressing issue that I must resolve immediately. Tell me, why do the People of the South have such wide feet?"

"I see you have yet another important question," Hillel said. "You see, my friend, these people live in marshlands and swamps, and this is why their feet are wide."

The man looked at Hillel in awe. "Are you not the great teacher, whom they call the Prince of Israel?"

"Yes," Hillel answered.

"Well, if this is the case, may there never be another one like you in all of Israel!" the man exclaimed.

"Why do you say this?" Hillel asked.

"Because on your account I have lost four hundred zuzim!" the man said.

"How can that be?" Hillel asked.

Shamefaced, the man told Hillel about his bet.

"Do not be upset," Hillel told the man. "My ability to be patient with you and with all people is worth far more than four hundred zuzim. You see, my friend, as long as I can demonstrate patience, I set a good example for all the world to follow."

[TALMUDIC SOURCE: *Shabbat 31a*]

Rabbi's Comment:

In Talmudic times, there were two great and opposing schools of learning in their interpretation and application of laws to everyday life. The school of Shammai was strict and unbending, whereas Hillel's was more sympathetic to accommodating the practical dilemmas of everyday life. In this parable, Hillel demonstrates that society is better served through tolerance, patience, and gentleness than by arrogance and inflexibility.

68. The Virtue of Silence

While Rabbi Yochanan, one of the most respected Talmudic scholars in Israel, was taking a nap, two rabbis waited patiently in his study. To pass the time, Rabbi Hiyyah asked his friend, "Why do you suppose there are so many fat chickens in Babylon?"

Rabbi Assi replied, "You call those fat? Why, I've seen many chickens that are fatter. If you come with me to the desert near Ghaza, I'll show you some really fat chickens."

Rabbi Hiyyah posed a second question: "Well, then, why do you suppose the Babylonians celebrate their festivals so raucously?"

"That's easy," Rabbi Assi said. "Obviously, it's the only time those poor people have any reason to rejoice. As their lives are sad and depressing, they celebrate their festivals in a big way."

"Enough of such trivial questions," Rabbi Hiyyah said. "Here's a really important question. Why do you suppose our peers in Babylon dress so much better than we?"

A more serious expression appeared on Rabbi Assi's face. "Well, of course they dress better. They feel they have to because they study at a lower level of scholarship than we do."

Rabbi Yochanan had been listening to the two young rabbis converse while he pretended to nap. He rose quickly and declared in a loud voice, "Such foolishness! Have you forgotten what I taught you? If you understand a question and have an answer, speak up. But in your case, Rabbi Assi, it would have been better for you to have remained silent than to appear so foolish."

Both young rabbis looked at their teacher. "Then tell us, Rabbi Yochanan, how would you answer these three questions?"

"First, the chickens of Babylon are fat because they have

never been deprived of food or fresh water. Second, the people of Babylon celebrate with abandon because they have not been subject to problems which could impede their happiness. Because they have always been happy, they have all the more reason to rejoice on their holidays."

"We understand, Rabbi. Now tell us what we really want to know: Why are the scholars in Babylon so well dressed?"

"This too has a simple answer which has absolutely nothing to do with poor scholarship," Rabbi Yochanan said. "The Babylonian rabbis were displaced from their homes and moved to other villages, while we have stayed in our own communities where we have already established a good reputation. Because people already know and respect us, we do not need to dress up in order to impress people. As you can see, our situation is quite different from that of the Babylonian rabbis, who are in a new country and dress in fine clothes to make a good first impression."

[TALMUDIC SOURCE: *Shabbat, 145b*]

Rabbi's Comment:

Rabbi Yochanan's advice emphasizes that it is better to remain silent than to provide an incorrect answer. The most interesting comment in this parable comes from Rabbi Yochanan, who addresses a popular international adage: Do the clothes make the man? The reference in the Talmud suggests that the sages believed perception was truth, at least as it appeared in the eyes of the general public.

And yet the quest for truth was foremost on the

minds of the sages. They were tireless sleuths seeking to discover and understand order in the foundation of the universe and human relations. Theological truth for them had to be God's truth, even as truth pertaining to the physical world had to be empirical.

69. The Siege of Jerusalem

Around the year 70 C.E., the siege of Jerusalem by the Romans was in full force. But Abba Sikra, head of the Jewish rebel group, refused to submit to the conquering Romans.

Seeing the slaughter, Rabban Yochanan ben Zakkai, Abba Sikra's uncle, sent word to him requesting a secret meeting. When they met, ben Zakkai said, "Our people are starving. We cannot hold out against the Romans much longer."

"What can I do?" replied Abba Sikra. "If I approach the Romans to protest, they will certainly kill me."

"We must devise a plan of escape," ben Zakkai suggested. "Perhaps I can rescue a few of our people."

"Let's announce that you are dying," the nephew said, "and everyone will come to express their sorrow. Then, when we say you have died, we will put something which smells foul in your bed to convince everyone. Two of your students can hide under the bed, and we will carry all three of you out of the city."

Ben Zakkai concurred. Rabbi Eliezer and Rabbi Joshua were chosen to hide under the bed. As the bed was being carried out of Jerusalem, a wary Roman soldier drew his sword and approached the bed.

"Do not pierce the bed," Abba Sikra said. "Otherwise, the Romans will think we have pierced our master."

Other suspicious soldiers gathered to shake the bed, and Abba Sikra spoke again.

"Do you wish the Roman people to think we pushed around our master, showing disrespect for the dead?"

Relenting, the Romans opened the city gate, allowing the bed to pass. Fearlessly, ben Zakkai went directly to the Roman camp to plead with Vespasian, governor of the conquered land.

"Peace upon you, O king," he cried. "Peace upon you, O king."

"I shall kill you now for two reasons," Vespasian said. "First, because you have the audacity to call me king when I am not a king. Second, if I were a king, why did you not come to me until now?"

"Even though you say you are not a king," ben Zakkai said, "truly you must be; otherwise, this great city Jerusalem would not have been delivered into your hands. You, Vespasian, are a mighty one, and the term 'mighty one' is a euphemism for king.

"Also, I was unable to greet you sooner because the rebel group barred me from leaving the city."

As they spoke, a messenger from Rome arrived, telling Vespasian, "Arise, for Caesar has died, and the Roman Senate has pronounced you their leader."

A jubilant Vespasian announced he would leave immediately for Rome. "I will dispatch a new governor to take my place; to you, ben Zakkai, I grant one request."

Knowing his request to save all Jerusalem would be refused, he asked, "Spare the people and the sages of Yavneh." This would enable the family line of Rabban Gamaliel to survive, and would include the physicians to heal Rabbi Zadok.

"If you do this, I will be content, knowing that I have done the best I could have hoped to do."

Ben Zakkai's request was granted.

[TALMUDIC SOURCE: *Gittin 56a*]

Rabbi's Comment:

How well Rabbi Yochanan ben Zakkai understood the need for drastic action during the desperate siege prior to Jerusalem's destruction! Thus, risking his own life, he managed to flee the city in the hope of reaching the rogue Roman governor, Vespasian. Certain that Jerusalem was doomed, ben Zakkai realized that to save the soul of Judaism, he must convince Vespasian to spare the population of Yavneh, particularly its children, and the wise men who would study and teach the Torah. He had accurately assessed that only this could enable Judaism to survive while the Romans enslaved the Jews.

Ben Zakkai's wisdom has paid off; while the Roman Empire collapsed and vanished, Judaism and its Torah thrive.

70. Sunrise, Sunset

Antonius, the great emperor, was pondering one of the mysteries of the universe. He summoned Rabi, one of the most brilliant scholars of the time, to consult him.

"Why does the sun come up in the east and set in the west?" Antonius asked.

Assuming that the emperor might have been jesting, Rabi countered with his own question, "O great emperor, if the movement of the sun was reversed, would you ask the same question?"

To that, Antonius replied, "My real interest is learning why the sun sets in the west."

Rabi answered, "We are taught that this is so the sun may greet its maker. Each of the heavenly bodies pays homage to God by its appearance."

"If this is the reason," said Antonius, "then the sun need only ascend to the vault of Heaven to bring greetings, and that would be just halfway. Then the sun could reverse itself and retreat. Tell me, what is the real reason?"

"Well then," replied Rabi, "the only other reason for the sun to travel across the entire sky must be for the benefit of travelers and workers. They know that when the sun has finished its journey, they may also end their journey, or finish their day's labor."

[TALMUDIC SOURCE: *Sanhedrin 91b*]

Rabbi's Comment:

Many rabbinic scholars of the Talmudic period had knowledge of various academic disciplines. But Rabi was aware that Antonius had access to the finest astronomers and mathematicians of his time. Therefore, Rabi probably surmised that the emperor wanted a spiritual rather than a scientific interpretation. If the Jews claimed that their God was the Creator of all things, then perhaps they also knew the reasoning behind these creations.

Hoping not to insult Antonius and to avoid possible embarrassment, Rabi initially responded with a simple message which contained a spiritual angle. He followed with a light-hearted reference to the order of the universe, in his mind attributable solely to God. Overall, Rabi acted cautiously, trying not to anger the emperor and avoiding falling into the trap of jeopardizing the Jews in the empire. Here we learn that one must always show deference to the ruling authority and capture the moment through wisdom and wit. Sometimes we gain greater security and acceptance when we appease those who attempt to embarrass us. Fighting back with sharp answers can only antagonize, while cool wisdom and reserve may sway others to our way of thinking.

FAIRNESS

———❧———

71. Enough Is Not Enough

A woodcutter carrying a load of firewood had stopped by the side of the road to rest. When Rabbi Ishmael happened to walk by, the man asked for his help.

"My load is heavy," the woodcutter said. "Would you mind helping me carry some of my wood?"

"Perhaps I can help in another way," the rabbi answered. "Is your wood for sale? How much do you want for the entire bundle?"

"You may buy it for half a zuz," the woodcutter replied.

"Here," the rabbi said, handing his money to the wood-cutter. "Now just leave it where it is. Since the wood belongs to me, I would like to give it to any poor person who needs it to build a fire and keep warm."

"Well, since I am poor," the woodcutter said to the rabbi, "I have the same right as anyone to it. I hereby claim all of this wood for myself."

The man turned to the rabbi and asked a second time, "Would you help me carry my wood?"

Once again, the rabbi handed the woodcutter half a zuz, but this time he declared, "I now proclaim that everyone has the right to this wood—everyone, that is, but you!"

With this statement, Rabbi Ishmael showed the woodcutter that good deeds performed out of love for others take precedence over profit or personal gain.

[TALMUDIC SOURCE: *Baba Metzia 30b*]

Rabbi's Comment:

Once a fair market value for goods or services is established, both parties should honor the agreement. They should be satisfied and stick to their contract even if a loophole that gives one party an unfair advantage over the other is discovered. This parable also reminds us that being charitable is a reward in itself, and sometimes the pleasure of giving is the most rewarding experience of all.

72. The Sale of a Ship

Rabbis Nathan, Symmachus, and Raba were engaged in a debate about which items are actually included in the purchase of a ship.

Rabbi Nathan said, "Certainly we can agree that the transaction always includes the mast, sail, anchor, and all the implements necessary for navigating the ship."

Symmachus and Raba nodded their heads in consent.

"Would the buzith always be included in the sale of a ship?" Rabbi Nathan asked his colleagues.

"Certainly," Symmachus agreed. "He who sells his ship includes the dugith."

Since the buzith and the dugith are simply different names for the dinghy, Raba interrupted, "A ship must have a dinghy to ferry people from ship to shore."

"Then we are in consensus that it's included in the sale," Symmachus chimed in.

"And do we have a consensus that unless specified by both parties, the sale does not include such items as the crew, the packing crates, or the ship's cargo?" Rabbi Nathan continued.

"Yes," Raba said, "however, if the seller stipulates to the buyer that the ship and all its contents are for sale, unless otherwise stipulated, everything indeed would be included."

"In that case we are all in agreement," Rabbi Nathan concluded. "No matter how we refer to the implements, unless otherwise stated, the expectation is that they are included in the sale of a ship."

[TALMUDIC SOURCE: *Berachot 32*]

Rabbi's Comment:

The rabbis of the Talmud were always concerned with fairness in business dealings. Buying and selling, borrowing and lending, and determining rightful ownership were issues that the rabbis routinely debated, reviewed, and settled. The goal of the rabbinic discourse on matters regarding the marketplace was to interpret the guidelines biblical text provided for daily life.

In this story, the sale of a property and its tangential accessories is in question. The rabbis concluded that all assets required to make use of the ship are included in the sale; items excluded, however, were those not required to operate the ship (i.e., the crew, the contents of its storage compartments, etc.).

The parable teaches us that the buyer and seller should scrutinize the terms of their agreement before the sale is consummated, to avoid potential conflict later. Misunderstandings can be averted by concise communication, and this is as true today as it was thousands of years ago.

In general, the Talmud strives to determine procedures and practices that are just and fair in commerce. The goal of rabbinic discourse is to interpret the guidelines of the biblical text as they apply to daily life.

73. Twelve Wells

All of Israel came to Jerusalem on a pilgrimage, but to their dismay, there was not enough drinking water to meet the demand. One Israelite, Nakdimon ben Gurion, approached a local landowner and bargained for use of twelve wells so the pilgrims could have an adequate supply.

The two men agreed that Nakdimon would replenish the twelve wells with water by a certain date; otherwise, he must pay a fee of twelve silver coins.

On the day of scheduled repayment, the landowner visited Nakdimon and demanded, "Either return the water or pay me the twelve silver coins."

Nakdimon countered, "We agreed that I have the entire day to repay you."

Afternoon arrived, and the landowner again approached Nakdimon. "I demand that my wells be filled with water or that I get the money owed me," he said.

Nakdimon reminded him that the day lasted until sunset.

The landowner retorted, "It is obvious that you do not have the water. I insist on being paid the twelve coins. The only way you can fill my wells by day's end is with a big rainstorm. But, we have had no rain for an entire year, and look—there is not a cloud in the sky. But if you must be stubborn, I will collect my money at sunset. For now, I plan to visit my bathhouse. Bring the money to me there."

Feeling depressed, Nakdimon went to the Temple. Wrapping himself in his tallis [prayer shawl], and standing before God, he prayed, "Master of the Universe, before Whom all is known and revealed, You know that I bargained for water out of honor to You, and not for any personal gain. I wanted it for the pilgrims."

Suddenly, the sky filled with clouds and so much rain fell that all twelve wells overflowed. The landowner rushed out of the bathhouse and met a joyful Nakdimon, just outside the Temple.

"Not only have you received your water," Nakdimon said, "but I expect you to pay me for the surplus."

"I am aware that the Creator of the Universe upset the natural order of things for your sake," the landowner replied. "But not only do I owe you nothing, I still expect twelve silver coins." Pointing to the sky he said, "As you can see, the sun has set, which means the rains came in my time, not yours."

Sadly, Nakdimon went back to the Temple and prayed once again, "Make it known that You, O God, indeed have beloved in Your world. Please respond to me again, O God, and thus make it known that You have those You love in this world." Suddenly, the clouds spread apart, and the sun beamed brightly.

When Nakdimon met with the landowner, he was told, "You owe me nothing. However, had the sun not appeared, I would have demanded the money."

[TALMUDIC SOURCE: *Ta'anit 19b*]

Rabbi's Comment:

In this parable, the rabbis wished to bring out the best in people by demonstrating that a deed which benefits others has more merit than one which reaps solely personal rewards. The value of doing a "mitzvah," or a "commandment" which produces goodness, is a theme that runs like a golden thread not only through the Talmud but through all of Jewish sacred literature. Although the Hebrew word *mitzvah* is often misinterpreted as a charitable act, the concept goes far beyond choice, which the word *charity* implies. Mitzvah incorporates the totality of the moral responsibility each person has toward another for the purpose of improving life and enhancing its meaning.

74. The Letter and the Spirit

Rab Hanan's son, Rabbah, hired a few day laborers to move some barrels of wine. While working, they accidentally dropped a barrel, which broke, and the wine spilled onto the ground. To punish the men, Rabbah confiscated their coats.

The workers went to Rab to complain about the way they were being treated. After listening to their complaint, the great sage advised his son to return the men's coats.

"But is this what the law would rule?" Rabbah protested.

"Do it in spite of the law," Rab replied, "and give the coats back to these men. Follow the path of goodness."

Once their coats were returned, the men said, "Look here, we are only poor laborers. We worked an entire day and we have families to support. Should we not receive payment for our labor?"

Rab said to his son, "Go and pay them."

Again Rabbah asked, "But what does the law require?"

"Do it in spite of the law," his father advised. "Maintain the way of righteousness, my son, and do not expect to always find life according to the letter of the law. Understand that the spirit of justice is often of greater value. Pay your workers anyway!"

[TALMUDIC SOURCE: *Baba Metzia 83a*]

Rabbi's Comment:

It did not matter to Rab that the barrel broke due to the negligence of these poor laborers. To the great sage, the matter extended beyond the issue of responsibility.

The important question is: Should someone of meager means be held responsible for damage incurred while handling valuable objects belonging to another? Is the responsibility for our possessions really assigned to others when we employ them?

In this parable, the argument is not whether the workers are exempt from the necessity to compensate Rab for their negligent care, but whether the employer should enforce restitution for valuables mishandled or neglected by those he employs, especially if the employees are poor: To enforce such repayment would be cruel, and avoiding cruelty is a value worth more than compensation for property lost; in this case the barrel of wine. In all cases, a good person goes beyond the letter of the law or the written contract to do what is just and beneficial to the other party.

75. The Buried Purse of Gold

A trader came to a village intending to buy and sell goods. Since he arrived a few days prior to a pending sale, this visitor decided to delay making any purchases until the commencement of the event. Meanwhile, he sold the goods he had brought with him, accumulating a purse full of gold.

It occurred to him that to carry such a large amount of money for several days could be dangerous. After some deliberation, he decided to bury his purse until the morning of the sale.

He searched and searched for a safe place, and thought he had found the perfect spot. In the pitch darkness of the night, he dug a hole beside a stone wall. He placed his treasure in the hole and quickly covered it with soil.

But when the time finally came to retrieve his purse, the man found it was no longer there. In distress, the trader sat on the ground and moaned, "What am I to do? That was all the money I had. If I do not get it back, I am ruined." While considering his options, he noticed that a stone was missing from the wall. This led him to conclude that whoever lived on the other side might have watched him bury the purse. If that is the case, he thought, what must I do to outwit this person so that I can recover my money?

After much thought, he came up with a plan.

The trader walked over to the nearby house and knocked on the door. When a man answered, the trader introduced himself. "I have come a long way to visit this village to attend the big sale," he explained. "I have a serious problem, and since I have been told you are a wise man, I am here to seek your counsel."

The man said, "What is your problem?"

"You see, sir," he answered, "when I came to this village, I was carrying two purses filled with gold. The smaller purse was filled with four hundred pieces of gold and the larger contained one thousand pieces."

"Please come inside," the man said eagerly. "Sit down and let me pour you something to drink. Then you can relax and tell me more so I can offer you my wisdom."

Once seated in the house, the trader continued. "I buried one of my purses in a secret place. I am, however, puzzled about what to do with the second purse."

"What do you have in mind?"

"Do you think I should bury my considerably larger purse of gold in the same place, or should I entrust it to a reliable person?"

"My advice to you, my friend," the man answered, "is to bury the second purse in the same place where you buried the first. After all, if it is a secret place that only you know, it will be very safe."

"That is good advice," the trader replied, "and I will follow it." He thanked the man and departed.

A few hours later, the trader returned to the hole where he had buried the purse of four hundred gold pieces. When he dug there, he saw that his purse had been replaced with all his money inside.

[TALMUDIC SOURCE: *Midrash Aseret Ha-Diberot*]

⟞⟋⟋⟋⟞

Rabbi's Comment:

You can outsmart a thief by appealing to his greed. Keep in mind that when a dishonest person comes across a windfall which he acquired without having to work, he will not be satisfied until he has even more. Conversely, a person who puts in a good day's work and receives a fair day's pay is likely to be content.

76. The Oath

During a period of severe famine that was followed by extreme shortages, a man gave a gold dinar to a poor widow and asked her to keep it for him. The woman hid it in a jar of flour.

Weeks passed and she simply forgot about the coin. One day, she poured out a mound of flour and, with it, the gold coin. Unknowingly, she baked the coin inside a loaf of bread. And when a beggar came looking for food, she gave him this loaf.

Several months later, the man came to reclaim his gold dinar. Frantically she sifted through the flour, but the coin was gone.

In tears, she told the man, "I cannot find your coin. It is not where I hid it." She said firmly, "I swear that I did not take it, nor did I derive any benefit from it. May death take one of my sons if I am not speaking the truth."

Within days, one of her sons died. When the sages heard this sad news, they were confounded. "How can this happen?" they challenged. "This woman spoke the truth, yet she was bitterly punished. What could she have done to deserve this?"

Then it was revealed that she did benefit from the use of the coin, because it displaced a minor amount of flour within the loaf, and this flour she was able to save.

[TALMUDIC SOURCE: *Gittin 35a*]

Rabbi's Comment:

The rabbis told this story to demonstrate the seriousness and consequences of taking an oath. This parable warns that one must be absolutely aware of all terms in a contract (or a vow) before taking it; a person's word was as solid as a written contract.

Surprisingly, the Talmud does not assume that a less fortunate person, such as a widow, deserved leniency. In instances when an oath was not made, a poor woman might have been spared such dire consequences. But, under an oath, there are no exceptions. As minor as her gain must have been, the woman actually benefitted from the coin.

77. The Scale of Justice

A wolf chased a fox through the forest. When he caught the fox, the wolf admitted that he hadn't eaten in several days and planned to devour him.

"Oh, so you are hungry?" the fox said. "Why didn't you tell me? It is not necessary for you to eat me. Come and I will take you to a place where there is so much food, you can eat to your heart's content, and never again will you go hungry."

The sly fox led the wolf to a well, which had a wooden beam at the top. Suspended from the beam were two buckets attached to both ends of a rope. The fox jumped on one bucket and descended into the well, thereby forcing the other bucket to rise to the top.

"Where are you going?" asked the wolf.

Pointing to a cheeselike reflection of the moon in the water, the fox yelled up, "Here, where there is plenty of meat and cheese. Get in the bucket and come join me in a delicious feast."

The wolf climbed into the bucket, and because he was heavier than the fox, down he descended, and upward went the fox.

The fox jumped to the edge of the well, and the wolf cried out, "How am I to ascend?"

"Ah," replied the fox, "the righteous are delivered from trouble, as the wicked fall to take their place."

[TALMUDIC SOURCE: *Sanhedrin 39a*]

Rabbi's Comment:

Told by Rabbi Meir, this classic fox and wolf tale goes beyond the simple lesson of cunning and naïveté to teach the importance of intellect and wisdom. The fox inquired and found the purpose of the wolf's pursuit. While addressing the wolf's need, the fox figured out a way to escape with his life. Knowing that he could neither outrun the wolf nor overpower him, the fox persuaded his pursuer to sidetrack a little. He knew that the wolf would be brought back up by the next person to draw water from the well, giving the fox an opportunity to escape and live another day, using his wit and wisdom to survive.

78. Bitter Wine

A horrible misfortune befell Rabbi Huna when all four
hundred of his wine barrels turned sour at the same time.
Losing one or two barrels was tolerable, but four hundred!
A calamity of this enormity requires discussion among the
rabbis.

Rabbi Judah, accompanied by a delegation of his peers, paid
a call on Huna. One rabbi delicately suggested that the misfortune might have been retribution for a bad deed.

"So are you saying that in your opinion I am guilty of something?" Huna asked.

"Is the Holy One guilty of punishing unjustly?" another
rabbi asked.

"If anyone has heard anything negative about me," Huna
pleaded, "please tell me now."

"Actually, we have heard that you do not give your tenant a
fair share of the clippings of your vines," one spoke out.

Huna did not deny the charge, but freely admitted, "This
may be true. But how can I share the clippings with him? The
man steals me blind. He takes everything that I do not observe
and divide."

Hearing this admission, the learned Judah now spoke. "You
have proven what we have always taught. 'Whoever steals from
a thief, gets a taste of it himself.' It does not matter if your
partner steals from you behind your back. That doesn't diminish your obligation to abide by your agreement to honestly divide your shares."

Realizing that two wrongs could not make a right, Rabbi
Huna pledged to give his tenant his fair share. Then some said
that the vinegar in his barrels miraculously turned back into

wine. Still others claimed that the price of vinegar shot up equal to the price of wine.

[TALMUDIC SOURCE: *Berachot 5b*]

Rabbi's Comment:

Everyone is subject to public scrutiny and held accountable to a higher source. In this parable, the rabbis teach that our deeds are rewarded or punished, even when we try to justify them by evoking the adverse actions of others. Still another message in this parable is that repentance is justly rewarded.

79. *Alexander the Not-So-Great*

Alexander of Macedonia visited a king in a faraway land. Wishing to impress his visitor, the king escorted him through a large storehouse filled with gold and silver.

"I came to observe your customs, not your wealth," Alexander told his host.

As they were talking, two men approached to have the king settle a dispute.

One man said, "I purchased a property of a ruin from my fellow here. While I was digging it out, I came across buried treasure.

"I told him, 'The treasure belongs to you. After all, I bought the land, not what was hidden beneath it.' But he refused to accept the treasure."

The second man cried, "I, too, fear being accused of robbery. I sold the property, which included all its contents and all rights of ownership from the very bowels of the earth to the height of Heaven."

"Tell us, our king," asked the first man, "what shall be done?"

After reflecting a moment, the king asked the first man if he had a son.

"Yes," the man replied.

The king turned to the second man and asked if he had a daughter.

"I do," was the response.

"Very well," the king concluded. "Simply allow your son and your daughter to be married, and give them the treasure. This way, they will live happily ever after."

The two men departed, and Alexander stood speechless.

The king asked, "Why are you so amazed? Do you disagree with my judgment?"

"Yes," Alexander answered.

"Then what would you have done had you been presented this situation in your land?" asked the king.

"In Greece," said Alexander, "I would have executed both men and taken the treasure for myself."

Upset by this reply, the king said, "If the sun shines and the rain falls in your country, it cannot be due to your merit. In fact, may the spirit of your soul be blasted out of you!" He dismissed Alexander and ordered him to leave his land.

[TALMUDIC SOURCE: *Tamid 32b*]

Rabbi's Comment:

The rabbis of the Talmud frequently used Alexander the Great as a character in their parables. He was portrayed as a "bad example," lacking the values they wanted for their students. In this parable, justice, fairness, and generosity are set against Alexander's narrow-mindedness, corruption, power, lust, and greed. The rabbinic interpretation would be that though Alexander conquered the world, his triumphs were only temporary. His shallowness and callousness would be remembered by future generations with dismay. In contrast, a person's good deeds will last beyond his or her immediate lifetime through lives of those who benefitted. And there is nothing more valuable than to be remembered kindly and respectfully.

SECTION III

—◆◆◆—

Our Covenant with God

Written by scores of pious rabbis, the following parables illustrate the need to make the presence of God a constant in one's life. These stories provide lessons epitomizing how righteous individuals devoted their lives to the Almighty with unwavering faith. Their belief in God was so strong, no power on earth could alter it. The lessons portrayed in these parables emphasize the benefits of abiding by God's guidance and divine laws. Clearly, it is not always the easiest choice to accept God's way—one's faith is tested often, and sometimes the dilemmas it presents are very difficult. And we have to keep the following lessons in mind as we go through life.

D E V O T I O N
80. The Burning Torah
81. Akiba's Imprisonment
82. Two Angels
83. Honoring the Sabbath
84. Reflections of the Divine
85. Temple of Gold

F A I T H

86. Caesar's Foolish Request
87. Thou Shall Not . . .
88. King of Kings
89. The Three Keys
90. The Most Precious Gift
91. The Flip Side
92. Another Time
93. Only for the Best
94. The Lamid Vavniks
95. The Coming of the Messiah
96. A Few Good Miracles Prove Nothing
97. When Vinegar Lit the Sabbath Candles
98. Honi, the Rainmaker
99. Who Brings the Rain?
100. Holy Sand
101. The Ultimate Test

DEVOTION

—⟨⟨⟨⟩⟩⟩—

80. The Burning Torah

Many Roman officials attended the funeral of Rabbi Jose bar Kisma, offering eulogies to commemorate his life.

When they returned from his burial, they found Rabbi Hanina ben Teradion sitting before a large assembly in the marketplace. Clutching a Torah scroll to his chest, Rabbi Teradion studied feverishly. Infuriated that he had not come to the funeral, the Roman officials ordered the rabbi seized and wrapped in the scroll he studied. Then, Rabbi Teradion was bound to a stake amid a pile of branches, which the Romans set afire.

To make the fire burn more slowly, the Romans placed wet wool over the rabbi's heart. Thus, Teradion would suffer and die a lingering death.

At the sight of her father's torture, Teradion's daughter cried out, "O Father, I cannot bear to see you in such excruciating pain."

"If not for the Torah scroll wrapped around me," Teradion replied, "it would indeed be hard for you, my dear daughter.

But as I am dying wrapped in this Torah, The Holy Blessed One, who is mindful of the Torah, will also be mindful of me."

One of his students shouted to Teradion, "Master, what do you see?"

"A miracle," the rabbi gasped. "As the parchment burns, the letters written on it are taking flight and soaring to heaven."

Another student yelled to him, "Open your mouth, my master, so the flames may enter, and you may die and end your suffering."

"May the One Who gave me life take it away from me," Rabbi Teradion cried, "but let no one cause his own death."

The executioner was so moved, he said, "Rabbi, I will raise the flame and remove the soaked wool, and hasten your death. Will you then vouch for me in the world to come?"

"I will," Rabbi Teradion promised.

As the flames devoured the rabbi's body, the executioner threw himself into the fire. Instantly, a voice from Heaven cried, "Rabbi Hanina ben Teradion and the executioner are both welcome into Heaven."

As the flames died, a weeping rabbi was heard saying, "Some take a lifetime to acquire a place in Heaven, and some acquire their Heavenly place in an instant."

[TALMUDIC SOURCE: *Avodah Zarah 18a*]

Rabbi's Comment:

Because of his unflinching devotion to God and the Torah, Rabbi Hanina ben Teradion's death has served as a role model for generations. His martyrdom defied the Romans and conveyed the message, "You may kill me, but you can never destroy Torah, which is indeed my soul." Torah, God's teachings of goodness, will never die, no matter how many Jews or scrolls are burned. The law for all humanity is eternal. The phenomenon of the burning parchment eloquently illustrates how the physical container may perish, but its spiritual contents, the characters of the Torah, are immortal.

This story of the hapless executioner provides another insight. The executioner was so moved by Teradion's display of unqualified goodness and loyalty that he was virtually transformed by it. It only takes an instant for a person's heart and soul to change. Goodness can instantly change an individual, perhaps altering the entire sequence of human events.

81. Akiba's Imprisonment

When the Romans banned the study and teaching of Torah in Israel, Rabbi Akiba was imprisoned for violating the law. Each day, Rabbi Joshua, a grain dealer, attended to the great teacher's needs. Most important, Joshua was responsible for carrying water to Akiba's cell.

One day, the warden decided that Joshua was bringing Akiba too much water.

"Why are you bringing in so much water?" the warden demanded. "Perhaps to weaken the prison wall so the rabbi can escape?"

With this, the warden dumped half the water onto the ground and ordered Joshua, "From now on, bring only this much."

Joshua carried the remaining water to Akiba, who said, "Joshua, I am an old man. My life depends on you; the Romans allow no one else to see me. Why bring me so little water?"

Rabbi Joshua explained.

Akiba said, "Well, then let me wash my hands."

But Joshua hesitated. "Rabbi, there is hardly enough left for drinking. Why would you use it for washing?"

"What am I to do?" answered Akiba. "We are commanded to wash; the rabbis say that transgression is punishable by death. Shall I overrule my colleagues and pay no heed to cleanliness? I am better off dead."

Akiba refused to drink anything until Joshua was allowed to bring enough water to both wash and drink.

When the sages heard about this, they proclaimed, "If Akiba, in the leniency of old age, was so meticulous with the law, how scrupulous he must have been in the zeal of his youth! He was so vigilant in prison, surely even more so as a free man!"

[TALMUDIC SOURCE: *Eruvin 22a*]

Rabbi's Comment:

The great Rabbi Akiba never wavered in his devotion to God's law and its power to bring goodness to the world. Nor would he ever abandon his belief that humanity had the ability and a responsibility to interpret God's law. Thus, even during harsh imprisonment, Akiba cherished God's law and his colleagues' interpretation of it. Akiba found death preferable to a life devoid of the dignity that God's commands provide. His devoted love and respect for both teachings and teachers serves as a model of human behavior for all time.

82. Two Angels

Rabbi Jose, the son of Rabbi Judah, is credited with telling the legend of two ministering angels.

One angel is good, the other is evil. On the eve of every Sabbath, the angels met a pious Jew leaving the synagogue and accompanied him to his home. When they entered his house, they observed that the lamp was already lit, the table set for the Sabbath meal, and the bed made with fresh linen. The good angel proclaimed, "May all future Sabbaths be this way," whereupon the evil angel was compelled to confirm, "Amen."

When the house was cold and dark, the Sabbath meal had not been prepared, and the bed was unkempt, the evil angel joyfully declared, "May all future Sabbaths be this way," and the good angel sadly agreed, "Amen."

[TALMUDIC SOURCE: *Shabbat 119b*]

———◦◦◦———

Rabbi's Comment:

The fanciful description of the Sabbath preparation teaches us the importance of this most special day of the week which represents God's joy in creation. To heighten our pleasure and appreciation of the Sabbath, we must begin in advance to prepare and welcome it. The house must be neat. The wine and bread must be ready. We might even invite guests to share our festive meal. Everything must be put in order prior to this special day of rest and refreshment so that we may derive its full benefit. This can effectively happen when we include the Sabbath and its preparation as part of our lives a few days in advance of its arrival. If we can discipline our lives and anticipate the joys of the Sabbath in advance, then good angels will accompany us as we rest and rejoice, and the evil angels will have no choice but to join in.

83. Honoring the Sabbath

Rabbi Eliezer and Rabbi Hanina were discussing the Sabbath and how it pays tribute to God, the Creator of all.

Rabbi Eliezer told his colleague, "The Sabbath should always be honored with a festive table setting." He allowed no exceptions, not even for a meal which is modest. "Even if a person requires only an amount of food as small as an olive," he said.

Rabbi Hanina agreed and continued, "Indeed, even though such a small morsel is consumed, the table should still be set as if a queen were attending with her royal escort. The Sabbath must be welcomed as a royal guest and should also depart with befitting accompaniment."

Both rabbis concurred that hot water and fresh bread is an appropriately soothing way to conclude the Sabbath. "Then," said Rabbi Eliezer, "until the next Sabbath, we may recall this one with delight."

[TALMUDIC SOURCE: *Shabbat 119b*]

Rabbi's Comment:

The Sabbath honors God and God's creation; hence, we must prepare for it properly. The Sabbath is sometimes referred to as "the Queen of Days," and for good reason: its gentle, soothing effect resembles a queen who dearly loves her subjects. Those who observe and honor the Sabbath are reassured that they will find rest and peace.

---

84. Reflections of the Divine

Rabbi Banaah frequently performed the task of marking and measuring burial sites and caves. This good deed prevented others from walking on or defiling the graves. Coming upon Machpelah, where Abraham had been buried for nearly 2,000 years, he met Eliezer, faithful guard of his master's tomb.

"For all these centuries," Eliezer said, "I have been honored to protect the final resting place of Abraham."

"And what has the great patriarch Abraham been doing all this time?" Rabbi Bannah asked.

"He is sleeping in the arms of his beloved Sarah," Eliezer said, "and she lovingly watches his face as she cradles his head in her arms."

"Please tell them that Banaah is waiting at the cave's entrance," said the pious rabbi.

Abraham overheard their conversation and called out, "Let him enter: there is no reason to prohibit him from seeing us asleep in each other's arms."

Rabbi Banaah entered the cave and inspected it, and then went on to the burial place of Adam and Eve. According to tradition, they lie entombed in an inner chamber of Machpelah. Banaah heard a heavenly voice: "When you saw Father Abraham, you gazed upon my likeness. But my image, which is of the Divine, you must not see."

"But I wish to measure and mark the cave," Rabbi Banaah said.

"There is no need," came the voice. "The inner chamber measures the same as the outer chamber."

Rabbi Banaah obeyed and did not enter. He did, however, catch a glimpse of Adam's heels. Afterward, he described the sight as "so wondrous that they could be compared to two glowing orbs, like the sun."

He also said, "Comparing Sarah's beauty to all others is like comparing a monkey to a human being. And Eve was that much more beautiful than Sarah. And Adam was that much more beautiful than Eve. And compared to the presence of God, Adam was as a monkey is to a human being."

Rabbi Banaah added, "To describe it more realistically, the glowing face of Rabbi Kahana was a reflection of the wonder of Rabbi Abbahu. And the glow of Abbahu was a reflection of our father Jacob. And the aura of Jacob was a reflection of the beauty of Adam, the first man who reflected the image of the Divine."

[TALMUDIC SOURCE: *Baba Batra 58a*]

Rabbi's Comment:

How beautiful it is to imagine the matriarch and patriarch of the three great western monotheistic religions lying peacefully in each other's arms throughout eternity! As this image of serenity transcends time, it reminds us that each individual contains a portion of the Divine and provides a vision of hope for all.

As Rabbi Banaah serves the departed by performing the sacred task of marking and measuring burial sites, he catches a glimpse of the Divine, and by his own description, it is more splendid than words could describe. He teaches that a portion of Godlike beauty exists in all human creation; although the ultimate

fountain of light exceeds anything we may encounter
on earth, a hint of its luminescence shines in each of
us, no matter how we may differ in comparison to one
another.

85. Temple of Gold

According to Rabbi Judah, the Egyptian Jews of Alexandria thrived under Greek rule, enjoying a sumptuous lifestyle, envied by all.

"If you never saw their synagogue," Judah told his fellow rabbis, "you have never seen the true glory of Israel. Their temple was constructed like a basilica. It had colonnades inside colonnades. And sometimes twice the number of Jews who left Egypt—over 1.2 million—assembled there.

"Inside, the temple had seventy-one pillars of gold, one for each of the seventy-one members of the great assembly," Judah embellished. "Each of these pillars contained at least twenty-one blocks of gold."

"This is incredible," the other rabbis said. "Tell us more."

"In the building's center was the bima, made of wood. The cantor of the congregation stood upon it, holding a cloth. At appropriate times, he'd wave the cloth to signal the assembly to respond, 'Amen,' to a prayer. Everyone would respond, 'Amen.'

"What was so remarkable," Judah continued, "was that the seats were arranged in a special order. People sat according to their occupations. The goldsmiths sat amongst themselves, the silversmiths sat amongst themselves, and so on with the blacksmiths, the millworkers, and the weavers."

"Was there a spiritual reason for this seating arrangement?" one rabbi asked.

"No, it was more fiscal," Rabbi Judah answered. "This way, when a poor man entered the building, he could recognize those of his own talent and trade. By sitting with them, he was able to meet successful people who could assist him. This enabled him to make a better living for his family."

"It all sounds so wonderful," the rabbis agreed.

At this point, Rabbi Abaya spoke out. "Yes, it was all wonderful until Alexander of Macedonia came and massacred all these Jews."

A hush fell over the group. Then one asked, "What was the reason for such a dreadful punishment?"

"They refused to heed the warning," Rabbi Abaya said, "never to return to Egypt after having escaped from Pharaoh. It did not matter that they returned under Greek rule—they were still sentenced to death."

[TALMUDIC SOURCE: *Succah 51b*]

Rabbi's Comment:

The Jews were instructed to remember their slavery in Egypt and were urged not to return to the place which forced it upon them. The organizational system at the synagogue was designed to eventually open up the opportunity for prosperity for all and it worked, but only temporarily. This parable is a reminder that the social structure, and others, that Jews design for themselves are likely to crumble under the weight of a regime which is inherently hostile toward them.

FAITH

———◆◆◆———

86. Caesar's Foolish Request

The great Caesar decided one day to confront the God of the Jews. He summoned Rabbi Joshua ben Hananiah and announced, "I desire to see your God!"

"You cannot see The Divine," Rabbi Joshua replied.

"Is that so!" retorted Caesar. "I will see God. I must see God. I demand to see God."

Hoping to appease the emperor, Rabbi Joshua asked Caesar to turn and face the sun directly.

"Look at the sun," Joshua said.

"I cannot," said Caesar. "It is too bright."

"The sun is only one of God's servants in this vast universe. If you are unable to look at the sun, Great Caesar, how can you expect to look directly on the presence of God itself?"

"Well then," said Caesar, "I will arrange a banquet for your God. Invite The Almighty to attend."

Rabbi Joshua simply responded, "It is impossible. Such a thing cannot be done."

"Why?" asked Caesar.

"Because God's attendants are too numerous."

"I will do it anyway," replied the emperor.

Caesar planned a huge affair by the sea, and for six months his servants labored. But right before the banquet, a strong wind swept everything into the sea. Then, for the next six months, Caesar's servants toiled, preparing a second banquet. Similarly, on the appointed day, torrential rains washed everything into the surf.

"What is happening?" the emperor demanded.

Rabbi Joshua explained that the wind and the rain were merely the sweepers and sprinklers that precede God. Caesar listened intently, and finally understood he would never observe the presence of God.

[TALMUDIC SOURCE: *Chulin 59b*]

———⟨∞⟩———

Rabbi's Comment:

The rabbis often found themselves in intellectual and spiritual duels with Israel's foreign rulers. Periodically, these foreign conquerors challenged Jewish beliefs. The idolatrous emperors ridiculed the Jewish faith in God and the Talmud refers to many instances when rabbis had to guard against offending their conquerors, who might respond with severe retaliation. As witnessed here, considerable diplomacy was required not to offend and anger Caesar. As this parable illustrates, Caesar is unable to win his argument against Rabbi Joshua and embarrass the Jews. Finally, Caesar is forced to concede and acknowledge that the greatness of God is beyond our comprehension.

———⟨∞⟩———

87. Thou Shall Not . . .

God had originally intended to give the Torah to all the people of the earth. In the beginning, The Holy One went from nation to nation, seeking acceptance.

God went to the people of Esau and asked, "Will you accept the Torah?"

"What is written in it?" they inquired.

"You shall not murder."

"No," they answered. "We live by the sword. We cannot accept the Torah."

Then God went to the Ammonites and the Moabites and asked if they would accept the Torah. And they asked, "What does it contain?"

"You shall not commit adultery," God told them.

"We are sorry," the Ammonites and Moabites responded, "but we have always committed adultery. We cannot accept the Torah."

Next, God approached the Ishmaelites and asked, "Will you accept the Torah?"

And they, too, asked, "What is written in it?"

"You shall not steal."

"It is our very nature to steal," God was told. "We cannot accept this Torah."

The reception was the same with all nations across the globe until God came to the people of Israel, who stood at Mount Sinai.

The Holy One held the mountain over the heads of the Israelites and asked, "Will you accept the Torah? For if you do, all will be well. But if not, this mountain will be your grave."

This time no one asked, "What is written in it?" Instead, they answered, "By all means, we will do it. Now, let us hear it!"

Questioning the true motivation of his ancient biblical ancestors, Rabbi Aha Bar Jacob asked, "But doesn't this story provide a possible excuse in our own day for not observing the Torah? Why should we embrace its teachings when it appears as if these commandments were accepted only under duress?"

In response, Rabba answered, "Perhaps; but as we know, ever since Mount Sinai our people have reaffirmed the acceptance of the Torah. In particular, what was confirmed in the days of Ahasuerus has been confirmed by every generation since."

[TALMUDIC SOURCE: *Shabbat 88a*]

———∽∾∽———

Rabbi's Comment:

This classic Talmudic parable described how and why Israel accepted the Torah. While most believe that the Israelites rejoiced at receiving the Torah, here we read of the possibility that they were as reluctant as everyone else. They refused the Torah until God persuaded them to accept it, but then they did so unconditionally.

With this interpretation, the rabbis teach an important lesson. They emphasize that the Commandments in the Torah are difficult to follow. Indeed, rejection of its decrees would have been easy. Yet, Israel has collectively agreed to live by the Torah from generation to generation. Why? Because at the core of our religious faith is the conviction that the values set down in the Torah are the ultimate truths which guide us in achieving the highest levels of honesty, personal integrity, social justice, and compassion toward God's creation.

And no matter how great our life's struggle may be, our commitment to the Torah represents our ongoing covenant with God and our willingness to accept The Divine will as superior and most beneficial to Israel and all humankind.

88. *King of Kings*

A pious old man was on his way home from a visit to a nearby village when he stopped by the side of the road to pray.

During his prayer, a soldier passed by and extended his greetings. The old man, however, did not stop praying to acknowledge the soldier's presence. This infuriated the soldier, who waited impatiently until the old man's prayers were finished, then began reprimanding him.

"You foolish old man!" the soldier shouted. "Don't you know your own teachings? Even I know that you have been taught, 'Take the utmost care to protect yourself, and for your own sake, be very careful.'

"And you should have been more careful. Surely, you must know that when you failed to return my greeting, I could have beheaded you with my sword. Why would you jeopardize your own safety by refusing to respond to me?"

"Do not be angry with me," the old man said. "I will explain: What if you found yourself standing before the king, and an acquaintance came along looking for a casual chat. Would you respond to this person?"

"Naturally, I would not," the soldier replied. "Certainly not in the presence of the king."

"What if you did? What would they have done to you?"

"Cut off my head," the soldier answered.

"Well then, I am sure you can understand my rationale," said the pious man. "If that is how you would have acted in the presence of a king, a man of mere flesh and blood, alive today and dead tomorrow, consider my options when you approached me. Think about how much more I was compelled to behave as I did when standing before the King of Kings, the Holy One, Blessed Be God, who is beyond eternity."

The soldier realized that the old man was right, and that he should not have been interrupted during a prayer. "I understand," he said. "You may continue with your journey in peace."

[TALMUDIC SOURCE: *Berachot 32*]

Rabbi's Comment:

This parable teaches that no earthly authority can compare to the power of God. Hence, when we are engaged in a prayer, no distraction should interrupt or intrude on this activity. Even when a tyrant offers us temporary security in return for our acceptance of his power, we must remember not to forsake our covenant with God.

Another reminder in this story is that religious faith ultimately triumphs over brute force. When religion is confronted by the sword, on some level it must never succumb, even when it is expected to. Only those who rely on their faith will truly feel secure. Sometimes we are forced into compliance in order to survive; and while we may have to manifest the compliance externally, it is the retaining of our inner, individual faith that will ultimately lead to salvation.

89. The Three Keys

Lecturing on the relationship of God and humankind, Rabbi Yochanan told his students that The Almighty kept three key elements of life closely held in Divine hands. "With each element," the rabbi emphasized, "God prevents any Heavenly host from acting as a Divine messenger."

"What were these three?" a student inquired.

"They were the keys to rain, to life, and to revival of the dead," he answered.

"What does this mean?" another asked.

"God controls the rain," Yochanan answered, "because the Almighty sees the watering of the land in its proper season as the best of all divine treasures."

Yochanan paused slightly, then continued, "The key to life is God's special gift. Just as the Holy One opened the womb of Rachel, our matriarch, so will God bless others with the gift of childbirth and new life.

"And with regard to the afterlife," he added, "God judges when to make the will of the Divine known, for it is when all graves are opened that the righteous of all ages will live once again."

"I have another question," one student said. "What is the key to gaining sustenance?"

"A very good question," Yochanan assured his students. "In my view, if there is rain, the hand of God is open, giving both wealth and gain."

{TALMUDIC SOURCE: *Ta'anit 2a*}

Rabbi's Comment:

From the rabbinic perspective, God can appoint a messenger to implement the Divine Will. At times, human beings may even be partners in divine efforts. This parable, however, suggests that God reserves the right to bestow blessings through rain, childbirth and even afterlife itself. This, the rabbis believed, is how God retains ultimate control of human well-being. Accordingly, God is always willing to hear prayers in order to respond favorably to the righteous. And, we are all entitled to rely on God's grace and mercy in response to our best behavior. This parable reminds us that the concepts of justice and mercy, as well as worldly prosperity, come directly from God.

90. *The Most Precious Gift*

On Sabbath afternoons, the great Rabbi Meir routinely attended the house of study to present his commentary to large crowds of students. During one session, his wife Beruriah stayed home with their two beloved sons. While the rabbi was gone, a horrendous tragedy occurred: both sons passed away.

Poor Beruriah was overcome with grief. In an effort to protect her husband, she carried both sons upstairs to their bedroom and placed them in their beds, covering them with sheets. She spent the rest of the day sobbing, waiting for her husband to return after sundown.

When Rabbi Meir came home following the evening worship, he inquired, "Why didn't the boys come to the synagogue?"

Unable to muster the strength and tell her husband of their loss, Beruriah beckoned the rabbi to sit down for the hot evening meal that had already been placed on the table. Beruriah thought it would be better to wait until Havdalah, the ceremony which concludes the Sabbath and ushers in the new week, to tell her husband of the terrible affliction that had befallen them.

"My dear husband," she said, looking deep into his eyes, "you are the wisest of all sages, so perhaps you can resolve a difficult problem for me."

"What is it?" he asked.

"Many years ago, some brilliant, precious jewels were given to me in trust. The owner placed them in my care, never intending for me to actually own them. Over the years, I knew that the jewels did not belong to me, and yet I became so attached to them, I knew that when the day came to release them, it would be more than I could bear. Now the rightful owner has come to redeem them. Am I compelled to give them up?"

Puzzled, the eminent rabbi looked at his wife, whom he knew to be an expert in the law, just as he was, and said: "My dear Beruriah, certainly you know the jewels must be returned."

Then Beruriah took her husband's hand and slowly led him to the bedroom. She drew the sheets from the bed and said in a soft voice, "My dear husband, as you have just spoken, all the wisdom in the world leads us to declare that we have no right to keep possessions that belong to another."

With tears in her eyes, she said, "It does not matter that we may grow fond of what is given to us in trust. Our beautiful sons were the precious jewels that God gave to us in trust, and now as the owner, The Holy One has come to redeem them. God has claimed what belongs to Heaven."

Rabbi Meir and Beruriah embraced each other, wept, and accepted their tragic loss.

[SOURCE: *Midrash*]

—⟨∾∾⟩—

Rabbi's Comment:

While it is always painful to lose a loved one, the loss of a child is the gravest of all. In this parable, Rabbi Meir and Beruriah are role models who display both wisdom and strength in their time of sorrow. Beruriah's compassion and sensitivity are demonstrated through the tremendous emotional strength she exhibits in her attempt to shield her husband from the shock of their loss. By the time she reveals to him the awful truth about their sons, the rabbi is prepared to associate his knowledge and devotion to the law with his own loss, thus enabling him to deal with the enormous grief he would have to endure.

Jewish tradition seeks to provide a coping mechanism to soften the impact of grief that accompanies the death of a loved one. The acceptance that each life belongs ultimately to God, no matter how attached to it we may be, provides some relief to those in mourning. Though we may feel a certain sense of possession of those we love, the time we spend with them is only a loan entrusted to us.

I frequently tell this parable to grieving parents who have lost a child with the hope that it may bring them some measure of comfort.

91. The Flip Side

While pondering the meaning of opposites in the world, one of Rabbi Meir's students inquired, "Why do you think the Holy One created a counterpart for everything in the universe?"

"Indeed, The Almighty created high mountains and low valleys; God made mighty raging seas as well as slow-flowing streams," replied the great teacher.

"Yes, that is true," responded the student, "but I was thinking about the way Rabbi Akiba once explained it. Akiba said that God created righteousness as well as evil. God is not only the Creator of the Garden of Eden, but also the Creator of the netherworld.

"Each of us has two portions awaiting us," the student continued. "One in Paradise, and the other reserved in oblivion. A pious, righteous person receives a double portion of reward, not only his own portion in paradise, but his counterpart's portion as well. Likewise, the evil, wicked person gets not only his portion in Gehenna [Hell] but his counterpart's, too."

Overhearing, Rabbi Mesharsheya asked if this conclusion could be proven.

He was referred to the Holy Writ, where the prophet Isaiah says of the just and righteous: "In their land, they shall have a double portion."

Likewise, the wicked are addressed by the prophet Jeremiah: "They shall be destroyed with a double dose of destruction."

[TALMUDIC SOURCE: *Chagigah 15a*]

Rabbi's Comment:

Each individual is free to exercise his or her own will, and for a particular path we take, each choice carries either a reward or retribution. Either consequence is a possibility, as theoretically, both Heaven and Hell await us, and at each juncture we are entitled to choose between doing good or evil. The rabbis believed that the double reward for embracing goodness was a compelling incentive for an inherently good person to strive to do the right thing as often as possible.

92. Another Time

There is a favorite story told by Rabbi Judah about how Moses ascended to Heaven. Moses came across the Holy One, who was drawing crowns at the top of the letters of the words in the Torah.

"Master of the Universe," Moses humbly asked, "why do You draw as You do?"

"Many generations from now," God answered, "there will be a man who will appear on the stage of history whose name is Akiba ben Joseph. And he will be so brilliant that he will be able to extract layer after layer of explanation from even the smallest part of each word in the Torah. This he will do even from these crowns which adorn the tops of the letters."

"Lord of the Universe," replied Moses, "show me such a brilliant man."

"Spin around, Moses," God said, "and I will show you."

As Moses turned, he found himself propelled far into the future to the academy where Akiba taught. Moses sat in a seat in the eighth row and observed as Akiba lectured to his students. Due to a language difference, it was difficult for Moses to fully understand Akiba's legal arguments, so he sat uncomfortably during the discourse.

But when the students asked Akiba about a certain law in the Torah, Moses perked up. "Master, how do you know this?"

"It is the law as given to Moses at Sinai," Akiba replied.

Moses found comfort in what he witnessed, and returned back through time to the Holy Blessed One in Heaven.

He was so impressed with Akiba, he said to God, "Master of the Universe, You have a man of such great intellect, and yet You give the Torah to me?"

"Be silent, Moses," God said. "For this is wha[t has] been ordained. It is your destiny!"

"Master of the Universe," Moses responde[d,] shown me a man with great knowledge and ability with Tora[h.] Now show me his reward."

"Spin around, Moses," God again instructed.

Once again, Moses was propelled into the future, and this time, he saw Akiba's flesh being weighed out in a meat market.

Moses was so horrified, he cried out in protest. "Master of the Universe, this is a man of such immense Torah learning, and yet such a horrendous reward!"

Then God paused and, looking up from the Heavenly scroll, said, "Be silent, Moses. This is what has already been ordained. This is his destiny."

[TALMUDIC SOURCE: *Menachot 29b*]

⟫⟫⟫⟫⟫

Rabbi's Comment:

Rabbi Judah's story about what Moses observed when he was propelled through time teaches a profound lesson. While Akiba was one of the greatest sages of the Torah, like all of us, he had a destiny that he could not escape. Just as Moses was destined to receive the Torah, so was Akiba destined to interpret and explain it. God's will and plan cannot always be explained or altered. While it is reassuring that a Divine plan gives us the freedom of choice, we are not empowered to solely shape our destiny.

As it is told in the parable, "The Ultimate Test," Akiba

was executed by the Romans because he refused to reject his study of Torah. Hence, while good people are subjected to ill fate here on earth, their ultimate reward comes afterward, in Heaven.

93. Only for the Best

Rabbi Huna told an old tale of Rabbi Akiba, who made a long journey by foot and stopped at a town to lodge overnight. None of the townspeople, however, would grant him a place to stay.

To an ordinary person, this would have been quite troublesome, but as a religious man, Akiba assumed that whatever the All-Merciful does, He does for the best.

The rabbi traveled with only three possessions of value: a lamp, a rooster, and a donkey. In a field outside the town, Rabbi Akiba settled down for the night. While he slept, a strong wind blew out the lamp. A cat crept up and devoured the rooster, and a lion killed and ate the donkey.

Undeterred, Akiba said, "Whatever the Merciful One does, it is done for the best."

That very night a band of thieves raided the town and carried off all the people. Had Akiba found lodging there, he too might have been abducted. Upon hearing the unfortunate news, he pondered, "Surely, I am sad for them, but their turning me away proves even further that whatever the Merciful One does, it is done for the best."

When someone asked Rabbi Huna to explain why Akiba considered this outcome for the best, Huna answered, "Had the light of his lamp been burning, the bandits might have seen him. Likewise, the rooster and donkey also might have exposed him. If so, he would have been abducted, too!"

[TALMUDIC SOURCE: *Berachot 60b*]

Rabbi's Comment:

This parable teaches that when divine intervention occurs, its consequences, regardless of appearance, can result in a blissful outcome. Whether we are able to understand it or not, God is ultimately merciful, compassionate, and just. Even though we may be unable to immediately discern this through human observation, a person of faith never worries or despairs of being abandoned, regardless of his or her situation. Instead, trust in God's goodness leads one to believe that the world, if not a particular individual, is reaping the benefits.

94. The Lamid Vavniks

In a rabbinic discussion defining the essence of a truly good human being, it was determined that every deed of such a person would be righteous.

"If only a single such person existed," Rabbi Eliezer stated, "God would have created the world for this individual."

"How could you substantiate your remark?" someone asked.

"Because we have learned that when the earth was created," Rabbi Eliezer answered, "God created light from darkness and saw that the light was good." This reference to the Torah stating that "the light was good" indicates that it was good for a good person.

Rabbi Hiyyah bar Abba quoted the teaching of Rabbi Yochanan: No righteous person dies and leaves the world before another such person is born to replace him. The rabbi explained that so few truly righteous people exist, that God dispersed them throughout the generations. Hence, the world continues to function for their sake, and their sake alone.

[TALMUDIC SOURCE: *Yoma 38b*]

———❦———

Rabbi's Comment:

An ancient legend says that at any given time, there are only thirty-six fully righteous and just people living among the entire world's population; these people are called the Lamid Vavniks. The number thirty-six is twice the number eighteen, which is the numerical value of the Hebrew word *chai*, meaning "life." It is

God's intention that the identity of these individuals be so well hidden that they themselves do not know they are among the unique group of thirty-six. The world really does exist for these thirty-six people; if not for them, God would have destroyed it. It is their actions and words which set them apart from the rest of the population. They never lie or slander or insult another. They would set aside their own personal needs and desires for the benefit of others. The Lamid Vavniks always act to make the world a better place for others and never seek personal gain at the expense of others' well-being. Their words and deeds are marked by a piety and devotion to a higher purpose, a perfect world of universal peace and prosperity. Each is the ultimate role model for human existence. Hence, whenever one of these special people dies, another is born to take his place, thereby ensuring the survival of humanity. The number thirty-six comprises two letters of the Hebrew alphabet: lamid, which has the numerical equivalent of thirty, and vav, which equals six. With these two Hebrew characters combined, we identify this special group of people, who by their righteousness, at any given time, save the world.

95. *The Coming of the Messiah*

Rabbi Joshua Ben Levi dreamed that he met Elijah, and as he had immense reverence for the prophet, Joshua dreamed that he approached him with apprehension to ask the question everyone wanted to know.

"When will the Messiah come?"

"Go ask the Messiah yourself," Elijah urged him.

"Where do I go to ask him?"

"Go to the entrance of the city of Rome," he instructed.

"And how shall I recognize him?"

Elijah replied, "He is sitting among the poor lepers tending to their wounds. He removes their old bandages and replaces them with new ones.

"The Messiah dresses and redresses each of their wounds with tenderness. He follows this procedure day in and day out. His concern is, 'Should I be summoned, I must not be distracted from what I do, because I don't want to disappoint any of the lepers for even an instant.' These are the terms you must comply with when you visit him, Joshua."

So in his dream, Rabbi Joshua followed Elijah's instructions and found the Messiah ministering to the lepers. He approached the Messiah with humility and a warm greeting, "Peace to you, my rabbi and teacher."

"And peace to you, son of Levi," the Messiah responded.

"When will you come, Master?" Joshua asked.

"Today," the Messiah answered, and they spoke no more.

Rabbi Joshua returned to Elijah and told him about meeting the Messiah. "And what did the Messiah say to you, Joshua?"

"He said, 'Peace to you, son of Levi.'"

"Good," Elijah said. "By those words, he assured you and your father of a place in the world to come."

"But he said he would come today," Joshua told Elijah, "and he did not come."

"Oh, Rabbi Joshua, it was not a lie," Elijah answered. "The Messiah spoke the truth when he said, 'Today.' He will come today—if only you hear his voice. That is the condition for his coming today. If only humanity would hear his voice."

[TALMUDIC SOURCE: *Sanhedrin 98a*]

Rabbi's Comment:

The Messiah awaits, ready to come at a moment's notice. But humanity is not yet ready. War, bigotry, hatred, indifference to the suffering of others, and the intentional infliction of pain—all these evils of the past continue to be the evils of today. When will we learn? Will we ever learn?

The Talmud teaches that although the Messiah believes in humanity, he knows that we are not yet ready for his arrival.

96. A Few Good Miracles Prove Nothing

In a "heated" discussion, a group of rabbis debated over the propriety of using an oven for baking. Did such usage comply with kosher laws? Some of the rabbis were convinced it did. Others were not.

Rabbi Eliezer advocated use of the oven, and he presented what he believed was conclusive evidence to support his case. However, his peers were unconvinced and challenged his views.

But Rabbi Eliezer believed he was right. After a lengthy debate, he pointed to a tree growing just outside the window and declared, "If the law agrees with me, let this carob tree prove it."

No sooner than his words were spoken, the tree jumped far away from its place! The rabbis could hardly believe what they had witnessed. Some estimated that the tree jumped a hundred cubits, and others even claimed it moved four hundred cubits.

When the rabbis calmed down, they huddled in a circle for a few moments. Then one of them said to Rabbi Eliezer, "No rabbinic ruling was ever determined by a carob tree. You have proved nothing, Rabbi Eliezer."

"Well, then, take a look at the stream that lies beyond the carob tree," Rabbi Eliezer responded. "If what I have said is in agreement with the law, may the stream prove it."

Just then, the waters in the stream reversed and began to flow backwards!

At first the rabbis were stunned, but when they discussed what they had witnessed, they reached a conclusion similar to their first: "No argument was ever proved by the waters of a stream."

While frustrated, Rabbi Eliezer was nevertheless determined

to make his point. "If the law is in agreement with me," he exclaimed, "may the walls of this house of study offer final proof!"

At that moment, the walls began to cave in on the rabbis. Rabbi Joshua intervened and scolded Rabbi Eliezer. "How dare you interfere with a law that was passed down to us at Mt. Sinai?"

Simultaneously, before he could finish his thought, the walls stopped their tumble—out of respect for the great Rabbi Joshua—and did not finish their collapse. But out of respect for Rabbi Eliezer, neither did the walls resume their upright position. So the walls of the great yeshiva have remained the same ever since—neither upright nor demolished.

As a last resort to convince his fellow rabbis he was right, Rabbi Eliezer called upon Heaven to help him win the debate. Just at that moment they all heard a voice from Heaven saying, "Why are you taking issue with Rabbi Eliezer? He is correct!"

Undeterred, Rabbi Joshua stood and announced to Heaven, "My fellow scholars and I cannot accept this. Proof of a ruling does not come from above, nor does Heaven intervene in our discussion. The words of the law have already come from Heaven. We received these sacred laws at Mt. Sinai, and they are to be interpreted by rabbis engaged in scholarly discussion, as we do now, not by invoking acts of nature. Therefore, we must let the majority rule."

Legend has it that shortly thereafter, Rabbi Nathan met with Elijah the prophet, of whom he asked, "Since the Almighty certainly heard the rabbis overrule Heaven, what was God's reaction?"

Elijah smiled and replied, "God only laughed and remarked, 'This is a time when my children got the better of me. Look here, they have defeated me!' "

[TALMUDIC SOURCE: *Bava Metzia 59b*]

Rabbi's Comment:

This classic Talmudic story illustrates the emphasis the rabbis placed on intellectual independence. The rabbis believed it was their right to interpret the laws of the Torah without intrusion from outside influence, even if that intrusion came directly from Heaven itself.

The law was given to the people of Israel at Mt. Sinai, and it is up to us to apply it in everyday situations. It did not matter that a highly respected scholar may be convinced that his beliefs are correct. A majority of scholars who remain unconvinced by Rabbi Eliezer's arguments would not allow any outside interference to persuade them. In any case, even the most highly revered individual may not always be correct in his interpretation of the Torah.

This parable also emphasizes that no rabbi is above the majority. According to the text, Rabbi Eliezer was censured for attempting to exert undue influence to persuade his colleagues. Their response sent a message that no rabbi should rely on supernatural forces to substantiate his argument.

97. When Vinegar Lit the Sabbath Candles

As his daughter was nervously lighting the Sabbath candles, Rabbi Hanina ben Dosa asked, "Why are you upset? This is the one night of the week when you should put your cares aside and let peace reign in your heart."

The young woman told her father that her distress resulted because, during her preparation of the Sabbath lamps, she had mistaken a can of vinegar for a can of sacred oil. "I fear the flames will die at any moment," she replied.

. Ben Dosa looked at the glowing wicks and assured her, "Do not be troubled, my daughter. The One who spoke has already assured that the oil will burn, and likewise God will make sure that the vinegar burns also."

And as ben Dosa had said, the vinegar burned throughout the night, and all the next day until it was time to bid farewell to the Sabbath and light the lamps of the new day.

[TALMUDIC SOURCE: *Ta'anit 25a*]

―◦◦◦―

Rabbi's Comment:

Acknowledged as a good and pious man, Rabbi Hanina ben Dosa often received special attention from Heaven. Some say it was his great learning that merited the favors he received from God. Others claim it was his innate goodness and ability to spread righteousness that placed him among those unique individuals who always seem to walk with God. Wherever ben Dosa went, peace and comfort accompanied him; he seemed to enjoy special benefits given to a man of great faith and love for God.

The mention in this parable of The One who spoke assuring that the vinegar would burn refers to the miracle of Hanukkah, when one small cruz of oil, enough for a single day, lasted for eight days. Likewise, we learn about the willingness of God to do miracles for Heaven's beloved. And, as one of God's beloved, Hanina ben Dosa was worthy of a miracle.

98. Honi, the Rainmaker

When the villagers needed rain, the order of the day was, "Get Honi the rainmaker," also known as the circle-drawer (see the parable "The Deep Sleep").

Once, the springtime month of Adar had nearly passed without a single raindrop. Honi was summoned to pray. And though he prayed, no rain fell. Recalling how Habakuk the prophet had brought on the rain, Honi drew a circle on the ground and stood inside it. In a raised voice to Heaven, he pleaded, "Creator of the Universe, Your children have called upon me because I am recognized as a person, who, within Your circle, has a special relationship with You. I hereby vow by Your great name that I will not step outside this circle until You show mercy on Your children."

A hush was heard from those who had gathered around Honi. Then suddenly, a few drops of rain began to fall. Someone in the crowd cried out, "Honi, our teacher, we look to you to save us from dying. However, this little bit of rain seems to be falling simply to release you from your oath. But it is not helping us."

Thereupon, Honi yelled to Heaven, "This is not what I asked for; I prayed for enough rain to fill every crack and crevice, cistern and cave."

No sooner than his words were spoken, the rain began to fall so heavily that it has been said each raindrop was enough to fill a barrel. Even the sages who have claimed to have seen everything were impressed by the size of raindrops they observed.

The strong torrents of rain frightened the crowd. "Our teacher, we look to you to save us from dying," someone said, "but this rain will flood and engulf the world."

Again, Honi shouted to Heaven, "I did not ask for this.

What I want is a rain that would be a blessing and benefit Your children."

With this pronouncement, the rain began to fall normally. But so much rain continued to fall that all the Jerusalemites had to seek shelter up on the Temple mount.

"Honi, just as you have prayed for the rain to start, you must now pray for it to stop," they asked.

He told them, "Although it is not my custom to pray to end an excess of goodness, I will on this occasion."

Honi then lifted his head to Heaven and said, "Creator of the Universe, Your People Israel, whom You brought out of Egypt, are unable to tolerate neither too much goodness nor too much punishment. When You were angry at them, they could not withstand it. When they received too much goodness, they could not take it, either. May it be Your will that the rains end, and that the world will be restored."

At that moment, the wind picked up and the clouds dispersed. The sun came out, and all the people headed to the fields to gather truffles and fruit.

[TALMUDIC SOURCE: *Ta'anit 23a*]

———

Rabbi's Comment:

The story of Honi is a classic rabbinic lesson that neither too little nor too much of a good thing is good. While Honi was able to fulfill the desires of Israel, the people were unable to decide how much rain they actually wanted. In this parable, the scholars ask the question, "What constitutes 'just enough'?"

From the human perspective, the practical amount

seems just about right. Yet, the rabbis teach that only God can ultimately determine how much is enough, and we depend upon The Divine to instruct us on what amount is sufficient.

99. Who Brings the Rain?

Hanan ha Nechba was the grandson of Honi, the circle-drawer. When a drought threatened, and the world needed rain, the rabbis would send small children from school to plead with Hanan.

The children would clutch the hem of Hanan's cloak and cry out, "Father, father, bring us rain."

Hanan would then pray, "Creator of the Universe, do this on behalf of those little ones who cannot tell the difference between the Father who brings rain and the father who does not."

[TALMUDIC SOURCE: *Ta'anit 23b*]

Rabbi's Comment:

This short parable tells us that no matter how miraculous our deeds may appear, ultimately it is the decision of Heaven to bring on a positive outcome. No human being can perform a miracle. However, the rabbis teach that all can indirectly bring on a miracle, because we have the capacity to call upon Heaven to work goodness on our behalf. The rabbis explain that while children may not be able to discern the difference between the petitioner and the doer, an adult should be able to make that distinction.

100. Holy Sand

To express goodwill toward the Caesar, a small Jewish village elected to send him a gift. A man called Nahum Gamzu, selected because he was an optimist, was chosen to deliver it. Indeed, his name actually meant, "This, too," because in every situation he would say, "This, too, is for the best." Some even believed that Nahum Gamzu could perform miracles.

Bearing the gift, Nahum Gamzu traveled until nightfall, then stopped at an inn for lodging.

"What are you carrying?" someone asked him.

"My village is sending a gift to Caesar," he answered.

Upon hearing this, some of the local men plotted to take the gift while Nahum Gamzu slept. They unwrapped it, removed it from the box, and replaced the gift with sand. Then they rewrapped the box and placed it beside Nahum Gamzu. After he woke up, Nahum resumed his journey, carrying the box of sand.

At the palace, Nahum Gamzu was granted an audience with Caesar. When Caesar opened the gift, he was infuriated to find only sand.

"Is this a trick?" he demanded. "Are those Jews playing a joke on me?" In a rage, he commanded Nahum Gamzu to be taken away and executed.

All Nahum Gamzu said was, "This, too, is for the best."

As he awaited his death, Elijah the prophet appeared. Disguised as a Roman, he went to the emperor and said, "O Great Caesar, you misunderstand. This is not ordinary sand. This is the sand of Abraham the patriarch. When Abraham threw this sand at his enemies, it miraculously turned into swords; when he threw chaff, it turned into arrows."

The Romans examined the sand and accepted its powers. And when Caesar did throw the sand at a neighboring enemy, the Romans conquered them.

So Nahum Gamzu was released from prison and brought before Caesar, who took him to the Roman treasury and offered him anything he desired. Nahum Gamzu requested only enough gold to fill the box he used to carry the sand.

Returning home, he stopped at the same inn where he had been tricked. The local townspeople asked, "So what did you take to the king?"

"What I took from here," he replied, "I carried there."

Then he showed them the box full of gold. They decided they too would take a box of sand to Caesar. Their sand, however, had no magic power—so they were hanged.

[TALMUDIC SOURCE: *Sanhedrin 108b*]

———❧———

Rabbi's Comment:

The eternal optimist, Nahum Gamzu lived his life believing whatever happened was always for the best. No matter how dire the events seemed, he believed that eventually they would result in a positive outcome. Nahum Gamzu placed total faith in God and exercised his own ability to seize the moment, fashioning the circumstances into fortune. Even his name, "Gamzu," in Hebrew means "this also" and implies "this also is for the best."

Today, such faith in God and in oneself is rare; but our ancestors lived with this strong, unwavering faith, and they managed to make the best out of even the most horrible conditions. If we could apply the same degree of optimism today, the world would be a better place; at the very least, it would appear to be.

101. The Ultimate Test

Nearly 2,000 years ago, the Romans occupied ancient Israel and devised a plan to destroy the Jews in a single generation. The government decreed that the study and practice of the Torah was forbidden. Teachers who violated the law received the death sentence.

Still, Rabbi Akiba gathered people into the public market and conducted Talmud lessons. Pappus bar Judah asked Akiba, "Do you not fear what the government will do to you?"

"No," the rabbi answered. "Because if we are forbidden to practice the Torah, it is the same as death."

Eventually, Rabbi Akiba was arrested and imprisoned. While he was aware that he would soon be executed, he never failed to say his evening prayers.

"Akiba," one of his students asked him, "how are you able to remain so dedicated to the Torah, even as you await your execution?"

Akiba replied, "All my life I have pondered this phrase in our prayers, 'We should love the Lord our God with all our soul, with our entire being.' For years, I wondered if I would ever have the opportunity to express such deep devotion. Now that it is presented to me, I do not wish to shy away from what I have looked forward to all my life."

The Romans did not extend mercy to Akiba, and sentenced him to a lingering death. But even as he was tortured, Akiba prayed to God. With his last breath, he uttered the final word of his prayer. Suddenly a voice from Heaven called, "How happy you are, Akiba, that your final breath would coincide with the words that affirm your faith." Then the ministering angels looked down from Heaven and proclaimed,

"What learning and what a reward! Akiba has found life everlasting."

[TALMUDIC SOURCE: *Berachot 61b*]

Rabbi's Comment:

This parable is the Talmud's classic tale of devotion to God. One of the most beloved sages of all time, Rabbi Akiba refused to allow the Romans to compromise his faith or the practice of it. Defiantly, he demonstrated his willingness to pay the ultimate price in continuing to teach God's word. This example was a remarkable lesson to his students, as well as to students in future generations: God expects us to live by the Torah, and to ensure by our deeds that others will perpetuate the values it teaches.

CONCLUSION

Our purpose in writing this book was to reach a broad audience of readers who have not had exposure to the Talmud. Since the actual Talmud contains volumes of information, this book is only a sampling of wisdom conveyed by the great sages over many centuries. If you enjoyed this book, you might want to study the Talmud—but remember that one doesn't actually "read" the Talmud; one becomes a student of it.

While the Talmud has mainly been studied by Jewish scholars, its wisdom is universal, without boundaries of religion, gender, or nationality.